PRAISE FOR
WORK LIFE WELL-LIVED

"The way we live and work is unsustainable. If we want to change that, we need to create human-centered workplace cultures. Grounded in research, *Work Life Well-Lived* shares a framework to help leaders prioritize people and focus on human outcomes as a measure of success, creating a more sustainable world of work for everyone, now and in the future."

—Jen Fisher, leading voice on workplace
well-being and human sustainability

"Before Kelly, I'd never read a workplace well-being book that was so realistic, implementation-focused, and balanced in both the business case and the 'no duh' human case. Whether you're an individual, leader, or strategic decision-maker, there's something for everyone in this book. Kelly took a workplace concept that's usually ambiguous, and made it actionable, with a splash of individual, team, and organizational accountability. I'm a tough critic when it comes to content that can impact mental health at work. I read this book faster than any other book in a long time, nodding my head the entire time, and having a good giggle too. A must-read!"

—Melissa Doman, MA, organizational psychologist
and author of *Yes, You Can Talk about Mental Health at Work:
Here's Why (and How to Do It Really Well)*

"Kelly Mackin has used her lived experience to develop groundbreaking research all in the name of helping individuals, leaders, teams, and organizations thrive at work. If you're looking for what's missing in your workplace well-being strategy, Kelly has the answers. Want to be empowered to create your most meaningful work life with health and happiness? You absolutely must read this book!"

—**Aoife O'Brien,** founder of Happier at Work and
host of the *Happier at Work* podcast

"Experiencing well-being at work isn't a 'nice-to-have.' It's a requirement for both individual and organizational thriving. *Work Life Well-Lived* is an inspirational call to action to fundamentally shift and rehumanize our ways of working. But more than inspiration, Kelly Mackin offers a research-backed pathway that demystifies well-being and provides tangible practices to rehumanize work."

—**Zach Mercurio, PhD,** author of *The Invisible Leader*

"In a world where burnout and dissatisfaction run rampant, *Work Life Well-Lived* offers an empowering guide to reclaiming joy and purpose at work. This book goes beyond the surface, delving into the core human needs that shape our well-being at work. Whether you're an individual looking for personal fulfillment or a leader striving to create a thriving workplace, this book provides the tools and insights to make it happen."

—**Simon Davis,** CEO of Purposeful Intent
and Future of Work evangelist

"I wish every leader and employee had a well-read copy of this book! If you want to become mindful of what matters most at work to you and others, this book is an essential read. Kelly Mackin provides a practical, evidence-based pathway and assessment tool for achieving genuine well-being at work. *Work life Well-Lived* illuminates the way to a purpose-driven professional life and a better future of work, one with greater compassion and human connection."

—**Suze Yalof Schwartz,** cofounder and CEO of Unplug Meditation

KELLY MACKIN

WORK LIFE
WELL-LIVED

The **Motives Met** Pathway to
No-B.S. Well-Being at Work

BONUS:
Includes a unique
code to take the
Motives Met Human
Needs Assessment

RIVER GROVE
BOOKS

Published by River Grove Books
Austin, TX
www.rivergrovebooks.com

Distributed by River Grove Books

Design and composition by Greenleaf Book Group
Cover design by Greenleaf Book Group
Cover image © Wes Henry

Publisher's Cataloging-in-Publication data is available.

Paperback ISBN: 978-1-63299-808-8

Hardcover ISBN: 978-1-63299-845-3

eBook ISBN: 978-1-63299-809-5

First Edition

To my mother.

May we build something brighter for the future from the hardships of the past.

There is no one I would rather pursue our dream of a better work world with.

This book is dedicated to you.

"A dream you dream alone is only a dream.
A dream you dream together is reality."

—John Lennon

CONTENTS

FROM ILL-BEING TO WELL-BEING

This may not be the first or only book you have read about creating a better work life, work relationships, or workplace, but I can promise you there is no other book like it. The years of research and truth finding we have done at my company, Motives Met, have led us to a completely new mindset and approach around what health and happiness at work is all about, how to get there, and why it's so important that we do get there. What we discovered is contrary to popular belief and the same stuff circulating on social media and the internet. Back in 2018, prior to the pandemic, we started to wonder about a few things; maybe they are things you have wondered about or struggled with too.

Why, after reaching the "success" they have hungered for, do people find themselves unhappy and unfulfilled at work? Maybe you thought, *yeah, if I can just find what I'm passionate about, then that quote "If you love what you do, you will never work a day in your life" will feel true,* and instead you find living your passion still feels like work—and not great work, either. Perhaps you've been seduced by the enchanting promises of social media influencers who insist that work-life balance and working from anywhere you want in the world is the answer to your problems, yet your stress and burnout is still eating away at you. You've heard the adage that "people don't quit companies, they quit managers," yet you know people who find themselves in a new job with a good boss and *still* dread going to work every day.

Why is it that you can be a leader who reads every damn book there is on leadership and follow through on all that advice, but your team still isn't engaged? You may have focused on growth opportunities or shared values, but you can see that unhappiness on your team is still running high. Or perhaps you've read new research claiming that connection and belonging are the most important factors for work culture, so you made those a top priority in your company, yet people keep walking out the door.

No matter the story or circumstance, what remains true is too many people feel their best work life is somewhere else—that it could be, and it should be, better than it is. Too many people struggle with their work relationships and company cultures. Too many leaders don't know how to create a great workplace where their employees thrive and thus their business thrives.

> Our own research at Motives Met found that only 16% of people are thriving at work. We can and must do better, because work is one of the most significant parts of our lives.

A statistic I've always found downright startling is that **on average we spend one-third of our lives at work. One-third!** Work has a huge influence over our holistic well-being, and yet it's one of the top sources for mental health challenges in people's lives. It's a breeding ground for stress and health issues whether physical, mental, or emotional. Your experiences, concerns, and emotions at work will bleed into your life outside of work and into the lives of those you care about. As Annie Dillard so eloquently put it, "How we spend our days is of course how we spend our lives."[1] Work life is life.

Ill-being at work still immensely overshadows well-being, and it's a disease that doesn't impact only an individual; it spreads to others, and we all feel the pain. Our work lives and workplaces are interconnected and interdependent. We all affect one another directly or indirectly. Working with or managing people who are stressed out, unmotivated, unhappy, not engaged, or just don't really care is not fun, and it certainly isn't positive or helpful for you. Unhappiness at work sucks all the way around: It negatively impacts productivity, culture, relationships, health-care costs, turnover, and performance.

Yes, well-being is "smart" in that it's tied to results. When you are well at work, you do better work. When your work peer is well at work, collaboration, performance, and motivation increase. When your employees are well at work, you are more likely to reach your strategic objectives and increase profit. From a business standpoint, a great deal of evidence shows that happily fulfilled employees are good for business, and the research in this book will further validate this truth.

Yet here is the bottom line: We all need to care about health and happiness, not only of ourselves but of the people around us. Not just because it's the smart thing to do—AND IT IS! But most importantly because it's the *right* and *human* thing to do.

Zach Mercurio, PhD, who is a researcher, consultant, and author of *The Invisible Leader: Transform Your Life, Work, and Organization with the Power of Authentic Purpose*, shines a bright light on this issue from a leadership perspective. He says: "Great leaders don't need a 'business case' to meet human needs like 'mattering,' 'purpose,' 'psychological safety,' 'inclusion,' or 'compassion.' Great leaders strive to meet these needs because it's the right way to treat people. The 'results' are a byproduct. We need to stop talking about basic human dignity by linking it to a 'business case' or 'performance outcomes.' When we do, we end up with buzzwords and tactics. Buzzwords and tactics don't last. We must work on fostering the *belief* that treating human beings well is a worthy end itself."[2] That is the work. It's evaluating the right things that matters.

Unfortunately, we aren't there yet. There is still too much convincing to be done for too many that well-being equals results (even though the proof is abundant and we will share our evidence as well), let alone that well-being matters from a purely ethical human standpoint. There is much work to be done, but my goal is that both the research my team and I have conducted at Motives Met and this book gets us closer, because the dream of a human work world is one we are wholeheartedly committed to. We know firsthand the toll that being unwell at work can take.

HOW IT ALL BEGAN

When I was ten years old, I walked into our kitchen one morning and, lo and behold, there was my mother flipping pancakes. My jaw dropped. This was not normal. This had never happened before school that I could recall. My mother didn't have time to be a pancake flipper. She was usually gone for work by then or frantically getting ready to leave for work. I asked her what was going on and she laughed at my bewilderment, telling me she had stayed up the entire night working and felt she had earned a break to make me pancakes. From then on it became more of the norm for my mom to be working into the wee hours of the morning and weekends spent chained to her computer.

I held such strong admiration for my mom. She was one of the hardest-working people I knew and was a badass woman trailblazer. She was senior vice president of research at one of the largest global creative ad agencies. She challenged the status quo, elevated how research was valued and utilized within the organization, and had a real strength for turning data into a story and insights into action. Other companies tried to poach her, as she was damn good at her job, but at the time she was pretty happy at work and didn't want to leave.

She loved—I mean LOVED—the work she did and was proud to work for a company that held a prestigious name in the industry along with the honor of working with some of the best in the business. Her company generously rewarded her financially and recognized the value she brought to clients. The work she did was creative and pushed the boundaries of the status quo. She had a gem of a boss who appreciated and supported her, and had enough flexibility to make her job work (as demanding as it was) with three kids at home. It was still one hell of a tough job that required much more than a 9 to 5; it wasn't perfect, but many of her important needs were being met and her job satisfaction was relatively high.

As a kid I would stay up late with my mom in her home office as she pored over data and research. I didn't get to see her as much as I would like, so this was quality mom-time. I set up my own desk in her office so I could "work" while she worked. I would draw and write, telling my mom, "One day I'm going to write a book." (Happy to say that finally has happened, Mom!)

I wanted to be there to soak it all in when she shared with me her presentations for Crayola or Disney. She asked my opinions to inspire ideas for her research. We discussed what made Gap cool—I loved the mellow yellow ads! We talked about how her research showed Dove deodorant was about to give Secret a run for its money. At this moment in time, the influence of emotion on our decision-making was met with skepticism, but my mom knew it was pivotal. It was vital, in fact. She pioneered a tool to quantify emotion and prove how emotions drive our behaviors with the ability to measure them in a validated way. She would often talk about her data on people's virtues, values, and mindsets and their impact on their behaviors. I was in awe of her intelligence, work ethic, and creativity; to me, she was the epitome of success. But the older I got, the more I started to see how her success eventually came with a big price tag—sacrificing her well-being and mental health in her overall life.

THINGS TOOK A TURN

Years later, everything changed after her company was bought out; all those needs that were met—feeling valued, working with amazing talent, doing innovative work, and so on—went out the window. A new boss came into the picture who was extremely passive-aggressive and made her life a living hell. She was drowning under the work that kept being piled on her, barely treading water to stay afloat without the ability to innovate and create. The talented people she enjoyed working with were either being fired or walking out on their own. She no longer felt appreciated, and it was clear her needs for stability and sanity were never going to be met. With the added pressure of being the sole provider for her three children, she felt stuck, beaten down, and lost.

It was devastating to see the work that had once lit my mom up and given her such purpose, joy, and confidence had now become the thing that was destroying her. On several occasions I could hear my mom crying before work, and tears would fill my eyes. One morning my mother wasn't just crying but she was physically ill due to the stress. It pained my heart so deeply that someone who gave so much, who had gone above and beyond for this company for twenty-five years, was being treated so poorly. Twenty-five damn years! I knew deep down in my bones this wasn't the way work should be, that it was just plain wrong, and yet I also held the conflicting belief, like so many others I know, that this was just the way it was. I thought I had to toughen up.

FOLLOWING IN MY MOM'S FOOTSTEPS

I ended up on the same path as my mother many years later as I began my career. I worked in the creative agency world, where I came upon the same sort of insanity. One company in particular was quite the chaotic, cut-throat shit show.

I remember a day that still stands out. I woke up in a panic around five o'clock a.m. to check my work email, only to find that my client "Hurricane Anna," as she was fondly called, had fired off nasty notes of disapproval for my team's work and issued a new, absurd twenty-four-hour deadline in the middle of the night. I spent the morning putting out one fire after another, adrenaline pumping through me as I jumped from one meeting to the next. Our company culture still reeked of the Mad Men era, but with a modern twist. Jameson whiskey had been poured at two p.m. to cope with a dreaded client status call. Full-fledged screaming was coming from one of the VP's offices. He was on a rampage again, yelling at one of the people on his team. And the creative director on my account had called me an "ice queen" because she was angry that a client had taken her off a project. The respect and connection among work peers was low, to say the least.

It was a long day that turned into night, and I found myself running through the streets of Chicago trying to make the last train home after work. It was the bone-chilling kind of cold outside, below zero, with the wind gusting in my face as I tried to half run, half walk in my heels so I didn't slip on the ice. As I approached the track at Union Station, I saw the train pulling away. Damn it. It was eleven p.m., I had left the house at six thirty that morning, and I still hadn't accomplished what I needed to for that day.

With the last train gone, I hopped in a cab for the not-so-cheap ride forty minutes out to the suburbs. On that ride home I can vividly remember how exhausted I felt. Not just physically exhausted but the bone-tired, soul-tired, burnout kind of exhaustion. And the kicker was: This wasn't even an atypical day. It was a shitty one for sure, but shitty days were not the exception at this job.

The sad part is I wore the title of workaholic like a badge of honor. The more I worked, the more I sacrificed, and the more I put up with, the more "deserving" I was of success, health, and happiness down the road, right? It was a small company, but I rose fast through the ranks with several promotions. I was a leader and "on the path to success," destined to be a VP one day as my mom was, I was often told.

But, similar to my mother, my health began deteriorating physically, mentally, and emotionally. I wanted to quit smoking but would cave due to the stress at work. The lack of sleep, constant rush, ever-present office drinking culture, and regular pops of Adderall to keep up only perpetuated the serious anxiety issues I developed. I started having panic attacks, and the stress often caused my left eye to twitch and my hands to shake. I was also struggling with stressors in my personal life, but I had no time to tend to them.

As a result of all this madness, my confidence was shattered. I had developed a sleep disorder and was dependent on sleeping pills. I fell into a dark hole that would take years for me to crawl out of—with the help of therapy and meditation. But the post-traumatic stress would linger for years to come.

A NEW WAY FORWARD

Looking back, I can clearly see that was insanity! But it's sometimes difficult to recognize how toxic our environment is in the moment, particularly when unhealthy work norms are encouraged, practiced, or even required by leaders. It's also what I observed during a portion of my life growing up; sadly, too much of it appeared normal to me. It seems so obvious now on the other side—doesn't it always? But at that time, I needed to wake up and get clarity.

I realized my health and happiness needed to be a priority in all areas of my life. And what exactly did that mean for my work life?

For one thing, I knew I had to stop believing that to be success-ful I had to accept being chronically stressed out, burnt out, and physically distressed. Beyond that, I realized that it also meant that the issues I cared about, that were truly important to me at work, needed to be in a healthy place—doing work that actually meant something to me, believing in the leaders I worked for, and having flexibility with options about the who, what, when, and where of my work. I needed to embrace a definition of success that was accurate and authentic to *me*, not one that was outdated and belonged to someone else.

I came to realize that being well at work wasn't just about stress and physical health, though that is a critical part. It was about having my most important needs met. And years later, that realization fueled the research that went into creating Motives Met.

You may not be living your "worst" work life as my mom and I were, but you may also feel you aren't quite living your "best" work life either. Your culture may not be toxic, but you may also know it could be better. No matter where you or your team or culture fall on the work wellness spectrum, meeting the human needs that matter most are at the heart of your best work life and workplace.

THE MOTIVES MET SOLUTION

I'm not going to tell you I have THE ONE MAGICAL ANSWER to achieving your greatest well-being or the well-being of those you work with or lead. Because the honest truth is there is no one right or "best" answer, even though there are plenty of people who tell you that there is.

What we have traditionally been taught about how to approach health and happiness at work is inaccurate. Yep, it's wrong. There is a lot of noise out there and an overwhelming amount of opinions, information, and advice that's often conflicting—whether it's from research studies, books, or CEOs of successful companies. This quote from the eminent biologist E. O. Wilson couldn't ring more true: "We are drowning in information but starving for wisdom."[3]

> In the pursuit of wisdom to make a real impact, our team at Motives Met dove into quantitative research to discover, "What makes a work life well-lived?"

Our solution is void of the B.S. of false promises of easy fixes and one-size-fits-all answers, because creating your best work life and workplace is tough, but that's why we created Motives Met—so we could make it easier, so we could make it better. What I do have for you is a path to lead you, five specific steps you can take with the insights and tangible tools we provide to get you to where you want to go.

THE PATH IS THE SOLUTION

In the chapters of this book I'll take you step-by-step down the Motives Met Pathway.

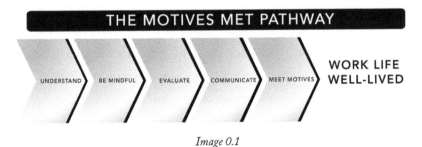

Image 0.1

We will empower you to: UNDERSTAND, BE MINDFUL OF, EVALUATE, COMMUNICATE, and ultimately MEET MOTIVES . . . to create a better work life for yourself, the people you work with, and those who work for you.

So what are motives? **Motives are the psychological, emotional, and social human needs that make up well-being at work.** Our research at Motives Met uncovered that there are 28 of these human needs (aka motives) that are the heart of health and happiness at work. Below is a snapshot of all the other tools, resources, and insights I am going to share with you. I designed this to be a book that you *do* as much as you *read*.

- Our **Motives Met Circumplex Framework** will provide a visually appealing and easily digestible way to understand the 28 primary work motives. For example, BELONGING, WORK-LIFE HARMONY, FREE EXPRESSION, GROWTH, FLEXIBILITY, PURPOSE, FAIRNESS, and SELF-ESTEEM are all motives. The 28 motives fall into ten overarching buckets or domains, as we call them, such as the Freedom Domain or Peer Connection Domain.

- **The Motives Met Human Needs Assessment™** identifies which five of these 28 human needs are MOST important for you personally to meet in order to live your best work life. Our research also showed that what matters most to me doesn't necessarily matter most to you. All motives matter, BUT they do not matter equally to each person or team. With the purchase of this book you will receive a free access code to take the assessment and uncover *your* top motives along with your personal Motives Met Report, which includes all sorts of information and guidance to help you strengthen your motives. **You can scan the QR code below on your phone or go to motivesmet.com/code to get your code and have it available for when you want to take the assessment.** You may take the assessment at any time, but I will formally invite you to take it at the end of chapter 3 once I have given you more context and background.

Scan below to get your free code.

- In each step on our Motives Met Pathway, I'll help you cultivate the **Motives Mindset,** which are the beliefs, thoughts, and attitudes to embrace to help you build the best collective work life for yourself and those around you. The data from our **motives research** that shows why motives matter in a big way will reinforce this mindset along with our **Work Life Well-Lived Principles,** which are fundamental truths to live by to keep these vital human needs healthy at work.

- Throughout the book I provide many **meeting motives resources,** like our **Motive Health Scorecard,** which will help you to evaluate the health of your human needs at work. This will also support leaders to develop simple well-being analytics to determine the degree that employees' motives are thriving or suffering. I will guide you to craft your **motive story** so you can reflect and better communicate with others and provide steps and resources on how to create greater trust and psychological safety so that honest, effective conversations around motives can happen in our work relationships and work cultures.

Last, you will use these insights to develop your **Work Life Well-Lived Action Plan** to meet your motives and, if you are a leader, your **People-First Action Plan** to create a culture where motives are met.

SHARING OUR STORIES

Along the journey, I will be sharing personal stories of people and leaders as a way to bring our pathway to life. For the sake of privacy and confidentiality, some of the names and examples have been modified while retaining the essence of the stories.

My own motive story is also woven throughout these pages. I am a white woman in her thirties who comes from a corporate background, and I recognize that while my experiences have their own challenges, my experiences and challenges aren't representative of those who are nonwhite, are members of a different generation, come from different walks of life, or work in jobs less similar to mine. It would have been impossible to include stories that cover all the vast job industries, diverse backgrounds, companies, and job levels, but I did my best to include the real stories I have that give a variety and also that best illustrate the concepts I am presenting.

FROM ILL-BEING TO WELL-BEING

Let me tell you a bit more about how I came to write this book. My wake-up call that well-being was the way, both at work and outside of it, developed a passion within me to not only pursue it in my life, but also to help others elevate it in theirs. Eventually, I walked away from my life as I knew it in pursuit of prioritizing health and happiness. I left my career in the agency world behind and moved from Chicago to San Francisco and then to San Diego. As I traded my office heels for hiking boots, and went from the pavement to the sand, I began to revive myself.

I joined my mom at the new research consultancy she started with another partner after getting out of her awful work situation in the advertising agency. I dove further into the world of research and insights on human behavior. I was driven to understand the effects of mindset on our lives and why we do what we do (and why at times we don't do the things we want to do!). Being so fascinated by my mother's research, I suppose I was destined to analyze data as part of my career. Numbers aren't my favorite thing, but I love gaining the insights they provide into pivotal areas in our lives, such as our emotional states, career, stressors, and health, and then using these findings to develop frameworks and models to better understand the world and ourselves.

As I studied human behavior and my desire grew to be a positive force for change, I wanted to understand the psychological and emotional side of things on a deeper level. Human behavior is an interplay between our cognition, emotions, and actions. To further understand this, I deepened my knowledge by studying cognitive behavioral therapy (CBT) and becoming an accredited mind management and CBT coach. I like to think of myself as a forever student of learning about the inner workings of our human brains and the science of how we think.

In my coaching practice I specialized in stress, mental health, and brain training. And wouldn't you know it—a common theme among my clients was that work was one of their greatest pain points and sources of anxiety, whether it was the lack of confidence they felt as a leader, their frustration with their gossiping coworker, the desire to "find their purpose," or the fears they were battling on their entrepreneurial journey.

Gradually my focus started shifting toward well-being specifically at work—issues like burnout prevention, using my "mind model" in the context of work-related struggles, and creating psychological safety. I found psychological safety at work to be so critical for mental health and positive work cultures that I became a certified practitioner so I could measure it, which I will talk about later in this book.

Many years ago when I was seeking out tools and help to gain freedom from my own stress and be the CEO of my mind, I stumbled onto meditation. I became a certified meditation teacher with Unplug Meditation and incorporated mindfulness practices into my coaching so that I could use it in a practical, modern way to improve life in and outside of work.

My past experiences led me to a moment where, as difficult as it was to leave the comforts of the career I'd built, I knew I had to be part of the work well-being movement because I knew I could help make a difference. We assembled a team and, using our team's background in research, human behavior, psychology, and mindfulness, we cofounded Motives Met.

In this phase of my career, I'm happy. Yep. Happy. Something that many years ago seemed so WILDLY and completely out of reach. My relationship with work is not only healthy, but my work life actually adds to the fulfillment I experience in my holistic life. It's not perfect, nor would I ever expect it to be (and spoiler alert: nor should you). But the needs I have that are most important to me are well met.

My emotional experience is balanced, where of course I experience stress, frustration, and overwhelm, but more often than not, I feel pride, contentment, and happiness.

Does a path to well-being exist that can get you to this place in your work life and help lead others to get there too? Yes, and this book will show you how.

WHO THIS BOOK IS FOR

I wrote these pages in dedication to my mother, a woman who was so committed and driven and who deserved better, just as so many of you reading this deserve better too. This book and the Motives Met Pathway is what I wish my younger self and my younger mother had had when we felt stuck, lost, and unwell many years ago. If you find yourself drowning in work misery where the Sunday scaries feel more like Sunday nightmares, this book is for you. It's also for those of you who feel positive about your work life but want to be intentional and proactive about your work wellness and continue to elevate your happiness in your career.

This book gives you a lifelong guide to help you continuously navigate the inevitable changes and challenges you will face as you build your best work life for years to come. It's for people who want to support the ability for others to thrive at work as well, and have a more authentic connection, or even just less tension, with the people they work with.

I first and foremost am writing this to you as an individual, as that is where it all starts. But here's the thing: To be a hero to the younger me, my younger mom, and any of you who want to have a work life that's well-lived, our solution can't focus only on you as an individual. It also has to include your coworkers, managers, clients, and companies, because we all impact these motives for each other.

WE NEED ONE ANOTHER, WHETHER WE LIKE IT OR NOT

A sacred truth we must rally around is that well-being is co-created; it happens when individuals, work peers, and leaders show up for themselves and one another in meaningful ways to keep motives healthy. To be honest, when I fully understood the depths of this truth, I didn't love it. At all. I didn't want to surrender to how much we need one another. And we do, in fact, need one another. Which is why it's so important to support one another's motives, to know how motives suffer and thrive, and thus how the people we work with suffer and thrive.

For leaders and managers, it's imperative to comprehend and care about each of the 28 motives, as you play a big role in the degree your employees will thrive. Part 3 of this book is here to support present and future people leaders. Even if you don't have a technical leader or manager title, you can still be (and for many of you, you already are) a significant influence on others. Anyone can impact culture; we all know how one person can change the entire dynamic of a team. It's beneficial to suggest ideas to your managers. Often you will also find yourself continuing to grow into greater leadership positions throughout your career, and having this knowledge will be invaluable. If you are looking for a new job now or will be in the future, having the understanding of what you want to look for in a boss—say, someone who will support your well-being—puts you in a more informed position.

I remember many years ago when I became a true manager for the first time and had no idea what the heck I was doing and no real strategy of how to ensure my team was happy and wanting to stay. I wasn't given any tools or coaching to help me, just as many leaders aren't—or, I would argue, even if they are, such guidance often falls short; that "once-a-year training" just isn't going to cut it. The Motives Met Pathway would have been so helpful for me to tap into on my own. And that's what I LOVE about our process: You can do it on your own, whether your organization has adopted it at scale or not. If you have a team of five people and you want you and your team to thrive, you can use the pathway.

Motives Met isn't just about the individual person; it's not focused on team relationships, human resources, or leadership; it's about everyone. That's why our Motives Met Pathway has the same five steps for all: It's purposefully designed to be walked together. You will see that's how I have approached the book, focusing on you as an individual, exploring interpersonal relationships, and then examining leaders and culture.

Ultimately, *Work Life Well-Lived* is for those who believe in our dream of a human work world and want to be part of making that dream come true. So without further ado, let's dive in.

PART 1

THE WORK WELL-BEING MOVEMENT

CHAPTER 1

DREAMING OF A HUMAN WORK WORLD

D ream with me for a moment. Imagine a human work world, one with true well-being to create a better collective work life and workplaces for all. A work world where health and happiness are treated as a right and not a privilege. One where all employees can show up as human beings with vulnerability and authenticity rather than trying to be unemotional robots who don't have feelings at their jobs. Where all of us have clarity on what we really need to create the kind of work life we want to wake up to every day.

Imagine there was a tangible way to determine what was working in our jobs, on teams, and in work cultures and what was not, so needed change could happen. Every person would feel empowered to take a proactive and preventive approach to their health and happiness at work instead of being on automatic or reaction mode in the day-to-day grind.

In this world, the relationship between a company and its employees would truly be a win-win for all. Employees would stick around longer because they genuinely want to, and deserving companies would have the ability to attract and captivate the best people. Leaders and managers could tap into their people's unique motivations with individualized considerations in a way that, well, actually works. And they would be given the tools they need to support, teach, coach, and inspire their people to thrive.

Organizations would have people-first cultures where employees' mental, emotional, and social health were true priorities. The diversity of people's needs would be respected and a mindset cultivated that elevated everyone's perspective on how they show up at work in a way that benefits everyone. There would be a shared framework and vocabulary to talk about stressors, concerns, and what we need to be well and perform well in a way everyone easily understands. People would see one another as human first and be able to create more genuine connections below the surface to make the sometimes difficult work relationships easier.

We created Motives Met to help make that work world a reality.

THE TIME IS NOW

I believe we are at a point in time when a significantly better world of work really *is* attainable. I don't use the word "attainable" lightly. Even when we started our research—before the pandemic—to create Motives Met a few short years ago, the dream seemed much further away. If you had told me then that "well-being at work" would be as hot a topic of conversation as it is now, I wouldn't have believed you.

Prior to COVID-19, there were glimmers of progress; the conversation had shifted from pure performance and productivity at work to satisfaction, engagement, and culture. And then it shifted further to include the most important things—a people-first culture, healthy emotional experience, mental health, and well-being. There was momentum, but the pandemic and the Great Resignation that ensued, with millions leaving their jobs in 2021, added fuel to the work well-being movement that was already under way. Now it has taken center stage like never before.

The pandemic was a time when many people had an opportunity to experience what a better work life would be like. It was a time when they could contemplate what it could be and start to develop a different mindset on what it should be. The Great Resignation is also referred to as the "Great Reflection." People had time to reflect and ask themselves, "Do I even like what I do anymore?" and start to explore work that would be more fulfilling or start a side hustle that grew into a legitimate business. They got a taste of what it was like to be at the dinner table every night with their family instead of sitting in traffic. Their interactions with their hostile coworker, hovering boss, or team dragged down by drama and negativity were minimized by working remotely. And hey, jumping onto a video meeting with a nice shirt on top and pajama pants on the bottom, with your dog lying at your feet, felt pretty good compared to a formal conference room.

A NEW BELIEF SYSTEM

Coming out of the pandemic, hearts and minds have been changed, and work life will never be the same.

> People have developed a new sense of awareness and belief around what they desire and deserve at work.

It's not just about their financial salary but their emotional salary, the nonfinancial gains that contribute to their job satisfaction.

Research has shown:

- 93% of workers consider their well-being to be equally critical as their salary.[1]

- 53% of employees are more likely to prioritize health and well-being over work than they did before the pandemic.[2]

- 67% of professionals believe that well-being at work is a right, not a privilege.[3]

- 50% of people believe their company isn't doing all it can to improve employee well-being and happiness at work.[4]

- 81% of workers agree that how employers support mental health will be an important consideration for them when they look for future work.[5]

- And it's not just lower-level employees, but leaders as well. One study found that nearly 70% of the C-suite were seriously considering quitting for a job that better supports their well-being.[6]

Not only did the pandemic change the work world as we know it, but technological advances, the rise of remote work, and the expanding knowledge economy were already transforming it. For many people, gone are the days where they have to live where they work. Same goes for skill set. Hate your job but feel limited in your capabilities or lack of formal education? No problem. You have access to online degrees, courses, and certifications; one could argue you could learn an entirely new profession—or at least a new set of powerful skills—on YouTube alone. Want to start your own business? It's far less daunting with the endless resources to help entrepreneurial souls venture out on their own and with the global marketplace connecting buyers and sellers from every corner of the world. The gig economy also offers another avenue for full-time employment alternatives. So yes, people will always need a job, but no, they don't have to stay in unfulfilling jobs with bad leaders or in toxic companies.

ENTER THE CHIEF HAPPINESS OFFICER

The expectations and power balance have indeed shifted, people are demanding more, and smart companies are paying attention. They are hiring new roles that never existed a few short years ago like global head of well-being, chief heart officer, chief purpose officer, chief connection officer, chief empathy officer, chief happiness officer, director of flexible work, head of people and culture, and VP of employee success. Prepandemic, the future of work was well-being; postpandemic, that future is already upon us.

My mom and I had known for a long time the work world needed to be challenged and elevated. We talked about the work world we dreamed of, the one we believed could be possible, but we decided we didn't want to just keep talking, we wanted to take action. If we had tried to create our company, Motives Met, with the mission to create a human work world twenty or even ten years ago,

I don't think we would have had a chance in hell. But today, enough progress has been made.

There is more wellness tech as well as more mental health programs, company culture books, and podcasts dedicated to this endeavor than ever before. I'm grateful that well-being at work has become a hot topic of conversation and for how far the movement has progressed, but work environments are far from perfect. Burnout, stress, loneliness, disengagement, and unhappiness have skyrocketed, and that was true even before the COVID-19 pandemic, before the world of work took another nosedive.

> Ill-being at work is still far more prevalent than well-being at work.

As I said, our research shows only 16% of people have strong well-being at work. Here's more data to back that up:

- Around thirty million US workers experience their workplace as toxic, according to research from MIT Sloan School of Management.[7]

- In a study by Deloitte, only 59% of surveyed employees said their well-being was good.[8]

- Consulting firm EY found in their research that 82% of people said they felt lonely at work and experience more loneliness now than before the pandemic.[9]

- According to Gallup, only 32% of employees are actively engaged in the workplace,[10] 60% are emotionally detached, and 19% are miserable.[11]

- A global survey from Future Forum found 42% of employees reported burnout—a record high.[12]

I wish I could say stories like my mom's and mine are things of the past, but that would be far from the truth. As people have shared their motive stories with me, I've gotten angry when a woman told me about her experience in a male-dominated environment being told she was taking too many "breaks," as they call it, to breastfeed. I've witnessed the frustration when a woman vented about her manager who insists on reading every single email she writes before she is allowed to send it. I've seen tears stream down someone's face when they told me about needing to take a year off of work and go to therapy because his boss was so emotionally abusive. Everyone has tales to tell of work wounds of varying degree from their present or not-so-distant past. I could keep listing more unfortunate stats and stories, but I think you get the idea: We still have a long way to go.

Along with the bad and the ugly, I've also heard about the good—tales that are uplifting and comforting. I've worked with HR leaders and CEOs who are working hard to create cultures where their people truly do come first. I've heard from someone whose company gave them all the time off they needed after losing a loved one. I've witnessed the feeling of belonging when someone was thrilled to find a position in their dream industry and was surrounded by "her people," as she called it.

These stories paint the picture of what's possible, of just how great work can be. Work can lead to fulfillment, fuel positive emotions, and provide many benefits. Even if it does simply, yet profoundly, work can support the life we want to live outside our job, or at the very least not stand in the way of it.

We have finally arrived at this present moment, where technological advances, a worldwide pandemic no one could have imagined, and shifting beliefs have made our dream possible in a way it never has been before. **The way forward is well-being, and every single day more people believe it, support it, and fight for it.**

WHAT GETS IN THE WAY: DREAM KILLERS

"What stands in the way becomes the way."   **—Marcus Aurelius**

This paradox was perplexing to us: With all the attention focused on work well-being and a better world of work and better intentions, why is ill-being still at an all-time high? Why are we still falling short?

We can't get to where we want to go if we don't identify the stuff that gets in the way. For the work world we dream of to become a reality, we have to eliminate the potential "dream killers," the obstacles that must be overcome.

We found there are ten major dream killers, and if we don't stop these threats, then our dream for the future of work will remain a dream and not a reality.

- Dream Killer #1: We don't really know what work well-being is.

- Dream Killer #2: We think we know "the answer" to what creates our best work lives and workplaces, but it's often not the "best" answer.

- Dream Killer #3: We push short-term Band-Aid solutions, but they don't work.

- Dream Killer #4: We don't know who to trust because of too many conflicting opinions and an overwhelming amount of information.

- Dream Killer #5: We don't bring our humanity to work.

- Dream Killer #6: We take a passive or reactive approach to caring for health and happiness at work, not a preventive and proactive one.

- Dream Killer #7: We don't show up in meaningful ways to co-create well-being at work together.

- Dream Killer #8: We don't evaluate and measure work well-being in the way we should.

- Dream Killer #9: We don't talk about what we need most at work with ourselves and others.

- Dream Killer #10: We don't prioritize health and happiness at work enough.

I will introduce you to each dream killer as we go through the book and discuss how we can eliminate them using the pathway. We must understand why we get it wrong before we can get it right.

At the very beginning of our pursuit to bring greater well-being to work, we started by asking ourselves the most basic question, "What really is it?"

Dream Killer #1:
We don't really know what work well-being is.

CHAPTER 2

WHAT IS WORK WELL-BEING?

When talking about work well-being, factors such as mental health, work happiness, and work satisfaction come to mind and can sometimes be used interchangeably or linked very closely when talking about this subject. These desired outcomes at work can be naturally ambiguous, a struggle to define precisely both generally and personally. I certainly didn't confidently know how to define being well at work, and I had never worked for a boss or a company that clarified what it meant either. Turns out, as I talked to people, I wasn't alone.

I searched for a definition of well-being I felt good about as a jumping-off point, something I could wrap my head around that would gratifyingly shed light on what it truly means to be well at work and thrive. But I came up empty-handed, in part because the context for work well-being could often be so vague. When you turn to the internet and scroll through popular articles or company websites, you will find that work well-being is "being happy and healthy at work" or "the health, satisfaction, and contentment employees feel at work." Chat GPT informed me that "well-being at work" refers to the overall health, happiness, and satisfaction for employees in their work environment. That sounds good, but what in the hell does that really mean? *How* do you do that? Sometimes there was no concise interpretation at all, just paragraphs of modern work happiness buzzwords.

It's not that being happy and healthy at work is "wrong"—I refer to that phrase all the time throughout these pages. But using these words alone doesn't help me if I am trying to figure out how to have a better work life. It doesn't help a leader figure out how to best support the happiness of their team members. Not without a "how." And most of these broad definitions didn't provide a clear how, a road map or framework to follow. Without that, well-being at work is elusive, fluffy, and intangible. If well-being at work is the goal, then lack of clarity makes getting it all that more difficult. The more we can all get on the same page as to what work well-being means in a more tangible way, the better off we will be.

When I searched across the internet for perspective, I came across more specific definitions and precise answers: Well-being is having growth and belonging at work, feeling appreciated, or having greater purpose. I then shifted from the internet and into the heads and hearts of people; how did they think about work happiness in their own work lives and workplaces? I asked individuals from entrepreneurs to entry-level workers to HR leaders how they interpreted well-being, and we also asked in our research. Some responses were general and some more definitive:

- "Not being stressed or burnt out and loving what I do."

- "When people have meaning in their work and employees feel safe and are treated fairly."

- "Being able to get my job done without costing me my sanity."

- "Having work-life balance and flexibility."

- "When employees feel valued and appreciated."

- "Being able to achieve my goals and innovate and create in ways that matter."

Were these people right? It's not that these more definitive answers are all wrong per se, though honestly for any given person they could be pretty off base. But are these statements potentially oversimplified, missing critical components to define a worker's happiest work life or not as spot-on as possible? YES.

AN INCOMPLETE UNDERSTANDING OF WHAT WE REALLY NEED

Dream Killer #2:
We think we know "the answer" to what creates our best work lives and workplaces, but it's often not the "best" answer.

Would less stress and more passion help your work wellness? Perhaps. Is that the complete picture or the best meaning around what you need or your employee needs to flourish in the biggest way?

Maybe not. It may very well be a half-assed truth, or it could be part of your truth today, but what about a year from now or five years from now? We are conditioned to think of happiness and well-being as a destination, a stop we get to where we never have to get on the train again. Once I have that salary that gives me the financial security . . . once I am treated fairly and respected . . . once I work somewhere I can truly create in innovative ways . . . once my schedule is more manageable . . . once I get to call the shots at work . . . then I will be healthy and happy.

Yet even after we achieve financial security, power, and fairness at work, we often find we still aren't happy—or worse yet, we're still terribly unhappy.

> Well-being is a journey, not a place to reach where we stop tending to it.

Sometimes the way we view our professional fulfillment can also become outdated and stale; we can have a fixed mindset that limits us when we don't update our thinking over time. It's tough to have an accurate vision of what your greatest well-being at work means today, along with the added difficulty of being open to change, paying attention to change when it occurs, and adjusting for it over time. The you of tomorrow may need different things than the you of today.

What also surfaced in our research is that important aspects of thriving at work tend to go missing. Reducing stress and feeling safe at work have commonly been associated with quality of work life.

I told someone recently I have a company that helps people create well-being at work. He said, "Cool. So you help people have better work-life balance?" That's another popular misinterpretation I hear *all* the time.

In recent years, flexibility and belonging have become a part of the "be happy at work" conversation. But what about being challenged, having fun, or being able to speak freely? While these might not be as commonly associated with work well-being, mental health, and happiness, we have nonetheless found as we dug deeper that they were, in fact, essential elements for some people to have their greatest quality of work life, even if they weren't always consciously aware of it.

LOST IN THE CHAOS

Our idea of what a fulfilled career or great company culture means is heavily influenced by what we have learned from others—what we see on Instagram, hear in a podcast, learn in a research study, or watch in a TED Talk. So, what were all these experts and influencers in the world saying about being happy and healthy at work? Let me tell you, our team had our work cut out for us as we weeded through the vast array of existing opinions, research, and advice out there.

Allow me to share some facts and figures relating to desirable work outcomes that are correlated and intertwined, such as happiness, retention, well-being, and performance.

- Researchers at the University of Birmingham Business School found that higher levels of autonomy lead to greater well-being and job satisfaction.[1]

- 71% of workers consider fair treatment at work to be of top importance. And employees who perceive they are treated fairly at work have 27% higher levels of retention and 26% higher performance.[2]

- When people feel like they belong at work, they are more productive, motivated, and engaged. They are 3.5 times more likely to contribute to their fullest potential, are linked with higher job performance, and are less likely to leave.[3]

- Of people changing jobs, 33% cited boredom and the need for a challenge as the primary reason for departing their job.[4]

- Employees who have a best friend at work are seven times more likely to be engaged in their jobs, produce higher-quality work, and have higher well-being.[5]

- 63% of workers who quit a job in 2021 cited lack of career growth opportunities as one of the main reasons they left their job.[6]

- Research showed 79% of people who quit their jobs cite "lack of appreciation" as a top reason for leaving.[7]

- 60% of employees consider coworkers to be the biggest contributors to job happiness.[8]

- Employee happiness increases as much as 20% by offering the flexibility to work 100% remotely.[9]

- 64% of employees report that trust with senior management is very important to their job satisfaction.[10]

- A study found variety increases happiness at work and offsets the potential for burnout or boredom.[11]

- 37% of American employees ranked "good work-life balance" as most essential to giving work meaning, more important than pay, praise, or purpose.[12]

- A Gallup poll of more than one million workers concluded that the number one reason people quit their jobs is a bad boss or immediate supervisor.[13]

- Research shows fun at work leads to greater engagement.[14]

- Research showed that across all levels of income, the most important factors determining job satisfaction were interpersonal relationships and having an interesting job.[15]

- Nine of ten workers will trade money for meaning. On average, they'd sacrifice 23% of future earnings—an average of $21,000 a year—for work that is always meaningful.[16]

Are you a bit drained from reading that list of stats? I know I was, and that only scratches the surface. I could fill up chapters in this book just talking about the data that supports how many different work-related needs correlate with things like greater happiness, satisfaction, engagement, productivity, motivation, loyalty, and well-being.

THE OPINIONS CONTINUE . . .

You may be familiar with the Gallup CliftonStrengths Assessment and Gallup's book *StrengthsFinder 2.0*. The book says that the key to being happy and engaged at work is utilizing your strengths, not your weaknesses. Gallup researchers found that people who use their strengths every day are three times more likely to report having an excellent quality of life, six times more likely to be engaged at work, and 8% more productive.[17]

Another book, *The 5 Languages of Appreciation in the Workplace* by Gary Chapman and Paul White, also offers an assessment, the Motivating by Appreciation Inventory. This book makes the case that appreciation at work is what we want and need most. The authors say, "The number one factor in job satisfaction is not the amount of pay we receive but whether or not we feel appreciated and valued for the work we do."[18]

Then there's social media. On my LinkedIn account I see a post and link to an article from a reputable online news source where an expert in the work culture space shares that "interesting work, relationships, and flexibility are top drivers of employee well-being at work." Then I'll scroll through my Instagram feed, where I'll see a video of a CEO with over a million followers pushing the message that you should do anything necessary to achieve your goals. "Hustle hard. Work hard. No excuses." The key to work happiness is growth and reaching your potential. Then I'll scroll further down my feed and hear just the opposite. "Screw hustle. You don't need to achieve to be happy. Prioritize calm not stress, your personal life not your work life."

Don't forget about the advice from successful thought leaders. In Steve Jobs's famous commencement speech years ago, he said, "You've got to find what you love. And that is as true for your work as it is for your lovers. Your work is going to fill a large part of your life, and the only way to be truly satisfied is to do what you believe is great work. And the only way to do great work is to love what you do. If you haven't found it yet, keep looking. Don't settle. As with all matters of the heart, you'll know when you find it. And, like any great relationship, it just gets better and better as the years roll on. So keep looking until you find it. Don't settle."[19]

Not to mention all the Band-Aid solutions: If you want to improve your well-being at work, you just need to use your meditation app! Take small breaks throughout the day! Take a walk outside! Eat a healthy lunch! Have better stress management techniques!

Let me tell you, when I was drowning in misery at work, I wanted to scream when I heard this kind of stuff positioned as a solution to my well-being woes. Walks outside and breaks are great. Self-care is necessary. *But* these things are not the cure for the major problems that obstruct well-being, even though we may wish they were because it would make life easier. Band-Aid solutions provide quick, simple answers to problems, which is why they can be appealing.

While these tactics or surface-level bandages can at times support health and happiness at work, bandages don't heal deeper work wounds that need stitches.

Dream Killer #3:
We push short-term Band-Aid solutions, but they don't work.

Band-Aid solutions include the free yoga classes or mental health day a company offers to show they care about their employees' health and happiness. One of my friends works at a large apparel brand that in 2021 gave their corporate employees a week off to "reset and recharge" during the pandemic. She said, "It was a joke and PR stunt, and everyone knew it. People are so burnt out and morale was so low on my team, it almost felt insulting that this was their solution. The week off was great, but as soon as I returned to work that Monday, the same problems were still waiting for me with no plan for resolution."

There are other surface-level solutions companies offer in hopes of creating an attractive cultural vibe and adding to happy work feelings—motivational speakers, wellness webinars, free happy hours, massage chairs in the office, and other perks, even financial ones. But again, if employees' motives aren't met, these superficial attempts simply don't matter. In an article by McKinsey called "The Great Attrition or the Great Attraction: What Will It Be for You?" the authors write: "Rather than take the time to investigate the true causes of attrition, many companies are jumping to well-intentioned quick fixes that fall flat: for example, they're bumping up pay or financial perks, like offering 'thank you' bonuses without making any effort to strengthen the relational ties people have with their colleagues and their employers. The result? Rather than sensing appreciation, employees sense a transaction. This transactional relationship reminds them that their real needs aren't being met."[20]

Offering free yoga or massages when people have no time to attend them isn't a perk. Giving wellness app subscriptions that won't rid someone of the stress from their micromanaging manager who doesn't give any clear direction or ownership over their work isn't going to work. Celebrating Pride Week but working with a client who is vocally anti-LGBTQ+ or recognizing Juneteenth as a paid holiday but only as a symbol while doing nothing substantive to support diversity, equity, and inclusion (DEI) or to rectify pay inequity isn't going to create real change—and your employees know it. Perks *can* elevate a people-first culture at work, but they have to be meaningful support versus fake fixes. They should reinforce and amplify what's already going right, not attempt to be a solution for significant problems.

CUTTING THROUGH THE CLUTTER

I don't know about you, but I find all of this exhausting. I'm left with a slew of questions:

- Can I self-care my way to work happiness?

- Should I focus on finding my purpose or using my strengths?

- If I don't find what I love and "settle," will I always be unhappy?

- Is the goal about calm and balance or achievement and ambition?

- Is there some ideal formula: belonging + appreciation = my healthiest, happiest work life?

- Can I offer enough perks to my employees to offset problems?

- If I focus on giving my team growth opportunities, autonomy, and flexibility, is that the best approach to keep them satisfied and thus keep them from leaving?

- Why does one research study find work-life balance or growth to be "the most important" but another study finds those factors are less important?

WHO DO WE TRUST?

After consuming all the noise out there, would I truly feel empowered to know my personal path to my best work life? If I'm a manager, would I know the steps to take to best support the happiness of my team? If I'm a CEO, would I have real clarity on the best way to reduce turnover and amplify well-being? Not quite. I may be overwhelmed as hell, and that's exactly how I felt when trying to make sense of all this information—overwhelmed.

The type A person in me was also *dying* for some sort of organizational structure that would make this all simpler to digest. When it comes down to it, who do we believe?

Dream Killer #4:
We don't know who to trust because of too many conflicting opinions and an overwhelming amount of information.

Sure, some of this advice can be beneficial and the stats insightful, but we need a way to organize, simplify, and prioritize all of it in a way that helps us instead of leaving us more confused or fatigued. And that's exactly what we did. We cut through the clutter to get to the truth of what it means to have well-being at work.

PUTTING INSIGHTS INTO ACTION
YOUR WORK WELL-BEING PERSPECTIVE

Take a moment to reflect on your own experience using these prompts, and then write down your answers.

- Have you ever worked for a company or leader who defined work well-being? How about what it means to have a people-first culture or happy team?

- How would you personally define work well-being?

- What do you think you need so you can live your best work life? What do you think others need? Is it the same or different?

- If you are a leader, have you ever provided context and perspective around what work well-being is for your employees? Why or why not?

Keep your responses in mind as you continue to read, and consider how your perspectives may change.

PART 2

THE MOTIVES
MET PATHWAY

UNDERSTAND

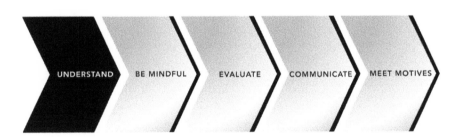

UNDERSTAND   BE MINDFUL   EVALUATE   COMMUNICATE   MEET MOTIVES

CHAPTER 3

THE 28 MOTIVES

The first step on our Motives Met Pathway is to *UNDER-STAND*. What was clear from the many conversations we had with others, all the research already out there in the world, and our own initial research was that we needed to get to the bottom of what it truly meant to be happy and healthy at work.

That's when we decided to go all in on our full R&D quantitative research. To dive deeper into the details, you can access our research report at motivesmet.com/research-and-approach. We wanted to figure out the elements that distinguished individuals who thrive at work—those who exhibit positive emotions, who are happy, fulfilled, and engaged—from those who do not share the same experience. After conducting over five thousand online interviews among US employees exploring emotional states, stress, behaviors, needs, and expectations, we found that people's personal work needs were at the core of their health and happiness at work. That led us to narrow our focus on studying human needs at work, and we explored hundreds of statements that would help us define what those were.

> What emerged from the data was that there are 28 distinct psychological, emotional, and social needs—what we call motives—that make up work well-being.

Our data grouped these 28 needs into ten overarching factors, or motive domains on our Motives Circumplex. See image 3.1, but our framework is so much cooler and easier to grasp in color; you can check it out at motivesmet.com.

THE 28 MOTIVES

"Understanding human needs is half the job of meeting them."

—Adlai E. Stevenson Jr.

Below is a condensed short summary of each of the 28 motives. You can find the full motives summaries on motivesmet.com/the-28-motives.

Success Domain

- ACHIEVEMENT motive

   I feel I am excelling at my job, achieving what I want to achieve at work, and I am reaching my current goals.

- CLEAR EXPECTATIONS motive

   I know what is expected of me at work, what I need to progress in my career, and I have clarity on what I need to do to succeed.

- PERSONAL STRENGTHS motive

   I get to do what I am best at in my job, and I use my natural strengths and abilities at work.

THE MOTIVES CIRCUMPLEX™

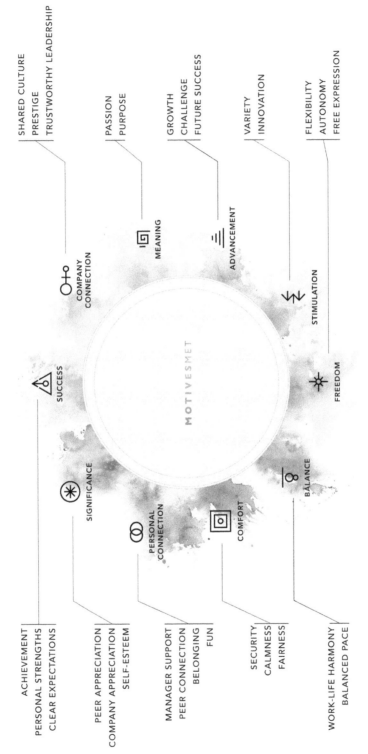

Image 3.1

Company Connection Domain

- SHARED CULTURE motive

  My organizational culture is a great fit for me. I feel good about their values and that I am more than just a number.

- PRESTIGE motive

  I get to work at a company that is trusted and admired by others, has a good reputation, and I work with high-quality people.

- TRUSTWORTHY LEADERSHIP motive

  I trust, admire, and believe in the leadership in my company, and I know that the leaders care about my well-being.

Meaning Domain

- PASSION motive

  My work is important and meaningful to me, and I feel passionate about what I do.

- PURPOSE motive

  My work is part of my bigger purpose; I feel I am doing meaningful work that matters to me and/or others.

Advancement Domain Motive

- CHALLENGE motive

  I have work that is achievable but challenges me and that is difficult but rewarding.

- GROWTH motive

  I feel I am growing to reach my potential, learning and gaining experience and knowledge.

- FUTURE SUCCESS motive

  The work I am doing now will set me up for the future success I desire, and I feel I am making progress toward my long-term goals.

Stimulation Domain

- VARIETY motive

  I have variety in my job, fresh experiences at work, and get to try new things.

- INNOVATION motive

  I get to be innovative and creative at work and am valued for new ideas and encouraged to come up with original solutions and ways of doing things.

Freedom Domain

- FLEXIBILITY motive

  I have freedom and flexibility at work and am able to decide how and when things get done.

- AUTONOMY motive

  I am empowered to take ownership of my work, make decisions, do my work the best way I see fit, and am not micromanaged.

- FREE EXPRESSION motive

  I feel my voice is heard at work; I am comfortable to speak freely and share my opinions without consequences.

Balance Domain

- WORK-LIFE HARMONY motive

  I am able to balance work and life in a way that feels good to me, do my job well within reasonable work hours, and have a life outside of work.

- BALANCED PACE motive

  I am not always rushed to get my work done, can work at a pace that feels good to me, and am given the time to do a job right.

Comfort Domain

- SECURITY motive

  I feel safe and at ease in my work life; have security, whether emotional, financial, or physical; and enough certainty and dependability.

- CALMNESS motive

  I am not stressed out at work; I feel calm and not overwhelmed.

- FAIRNESS motive

  My company treats people fairly, doesn't play favorites, is not biased, and judges people on their performance and nothing else.

Peer Connection Domain

- PEER CONNECTION motive

  I like the people I work with on a personal level, feel a connection, and get along with them.

- BELONGING motive

    I feel I belong at work and am accepted for who I am by the people I work with.

- FUN motive

    My work can be fun sometimes, not too serious, and I have a good time with the people I work with.

- MANAGER SUPPORT motive

    I have a great relationship with my manager; they want me to succeed and trust me to do my job.

Significance Domain

- PEER APPRECIATION motive

    The people I work with admire what I do and recognize and appreciate my hard work.

- COMPANY APPRECIATION motive

    My company recognizes my performance and rewards me for the work I do.

- SELF-ESTEEM motive

    My opinion matters at work. The role I play is seen as important and pivotal by others, and I feel I matter.

BUT THERE'S MORE . . .

While we can all require aspects of these 28 human needs to be well and perform well at work, we don't need them to the same degree, in the same way, or at the same time in our career journey.

The answer does not lie in rank ordering the 28 needs to create a hierarchy of importance, seeing which three motives rise to the top from a research sample, and then proclaiming that you should focus on these three needs the most to achieve your best work life. The reality is that a motive of top importance to one person could fall to the bottom for another person. PEER CONNECTION, for example, could be a well-met motive for you, but if it's not of significant importance to you and your other vital needs are neglected, then your well-being suffers. Same goes for a team. A one-size-fits-all approach is part of the problem. Clearly there needs to be a personal approach based on each person, each team, and each culture.

In our data, the top motives of each person were quite diverse. Each of the 28 motives was significant from a data perspective. Any one motive will appear in a person's most important motives for 25% or more of employees. While all motives matter, they don't matter equally to each person. Our data showed that a few motives rise to the top in importance and influence for each one of us at this present moment. **You will have optimal health and happiness at work when your top motives are protected, honored, and strengthened.**

Everyone's top motives are different, and they will also be different for you over the course of your work life. The first critical step is to get clarity on what those most influential needs are for you to focus on first.

> That's why we created the Motives Met Human Needs Assessment™: to uncover the top 5 motives that you need to have met in order to live your best work life.

When you take the assessment, you get your personal circumplex to see where you fall on the "motive map." Image 3.2 shows my personal Motives Circumplex. You'll see how my top 5 motives today are PRESTIGE, TRUSTWORTHY LEADERSHIP, FUTURE SUCCESS, FLEXIBILITY, and AUTONOMY.

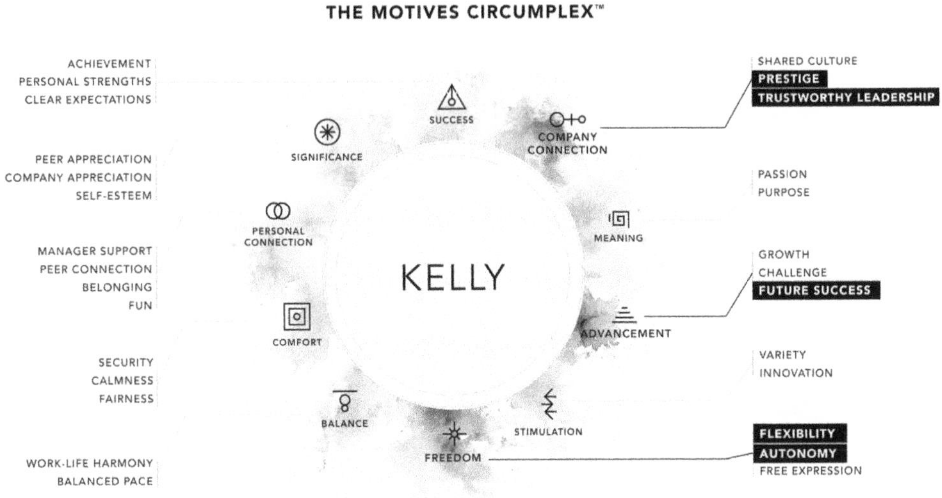

THE MOTIVES CIRCUMPLEX™

Image 3.2 Kelly Mackin's Motives Circumplex 2024

This will come to life better when you see it in color in the Motives Met Report you receive after taking the assessment, as all the areas that are not part of your top motives are grayed out and only your specific motive areas will clearly pop out in color.

There are five main takeaways I want you to grasp.

TAKEAWAY #1: YOU MUST LIVE IN THE TENSION OF THESE NEEDS WELL

Motives can hold friction with one another. Motives next to one another on the Motives Circumplex have a high correlation, while motives across from one another are less likely to be correlated.

Domains across from one another and the motives within them are not "opposites" necessarily, but there can be more of a dynamic tension between them.

Motives Further Apart May Hold More Tension

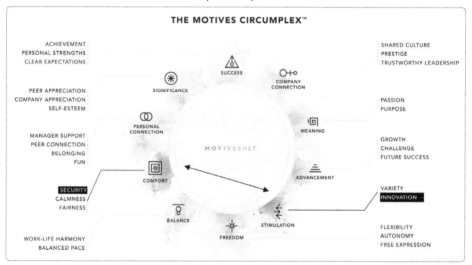

Motives in Closer Proximity Have More in Common

Image 3.3

Trying to meet motives that are spread out may at times be a source of internal or external friction, but this scenario happens quite frequently. For example, internally you may feel a push and pull between trying to satisfy your need for using your PERSONAL STRENGTHS and having CLEAR EXPECTATIONS, along with your need to have the FUTURE SUCCESS you desire that requires you to rise to a CHALLENGE and stretch outside your natural capabilities.

Person A, for example, might be driven toward meeting needs such as PEER CONNECTION, BELONGING, and PEER APPRECIATION on the left upper side of the Motives Circumplex. But Person B could have needs in the lower-right side such as INNOVATION, AUTONOMY, and FREE EXPRESSION that are more important.

Tension might arise when Person A wants more group meetings and collaboration, while Person B wants to limit meetings and own their part of the project solo. Person A thrives in an environment of recognition, focusing on what everyone is excelling at, while Person B might not tend to vocalize or give praise as often, but rather emphasize areas where the team needs to grow in order to develop more creative original solutions.

The truth of this tension between motives means that you need to give up the unrealistic notion of perfection. You will need to accept that two motives may not be able to thrive equally for you at the same time. On your team or in your organization, motives will not all be thriving simultaneously. You will need to compromise, and people who work together will need to compromise. Tough choices will need to be made. It is not about perfection; it's about optimization.

TAKEAWAY #2: NOURISH PERSONAL TOP NEEDS FIRST

Our framework in and of itself is extremely powerful. It gives you a clear, organized picture of the 28 human needs that are the foundation to a thriving work life and work culture. Hallelujah for some organizational structure! It fuels the desired mindset that all of these psychological, emotional, and social needs are powerful and worthy and need to be supported in the workplace.

This is not to say you disregard all other motives that aren't in your top 5. If some of these were better met, they could be well-being amplifiers, and if not met, well-being soul crushers. But the million-dollar question is, "Are my top motives met?" There is no fixed hierarchy of needs; it's discovering what your needs hierarchy is. You must focus on nourishing your dominant needs first while having greater awareness of the other human needs that impact health and happiness at work for yourself and others.

MOTIVES WILL VARY IN IMPORTANCE

Just because a motive isn't in someone's top 5 doesn't mean they find it unimportant. Some motives you may truthfully find to be of less importance or not as relevant to you.

For example, I mentioned two other assessments in the last chapter, the Gallup StrengthsFinder Assessment and the Motivating by Appreciation Inventory. Do I believe we will be more fulfilled if we know our strengths and get to focus on our natural abilities at work rather than our weakness, as StrengthsFinder claims? Yes, I definitely do. Do I think appreciation is important and, as the *5 Languages of Appreciation in the Workplace* book indicates, it's helpful to know how people we work with like to feel appreciated? Absolutely! I appreciate the research and insights behind these two tools and the value they bring to teams at work. And yet these three motives—PERSONAL STRENGTHS, PEER APPRECIATION, and COMPANY APPRECIATION—are not close to being of top importance for me personally to be happy and healthy at work.

For example, as I created and built Motives Met, I have had to wear many hats and take on tasks and responsibilities that are not my forte in the slightest, including some that I downright hated. It would have been a benefit for sure to operate more in my strengths, but that didn't have a perilous impact on my well-being. For someone else who greatly needs to operate in their strengths zone, it would have had a much worse effect. If the needs lacking in your work life aren't a top priority, this scenario is not going to affect you as much as if you lack items that *are* top priorities. Sometimes if a motive is lacking too much and also is important enough, that can be a reason it becomes a higher priority.

WORK-LIFE HARMONY is also not one of my top motives, but that doesn't mean I don't care about it—I certainly do! Yet I could have all the harmony and balance in the world between my work and personal life, but if I do not feel I am setting myself up for FUTURE SUCCESS (one of my top motives) to reach my professional goals, my well-being will take a downturn; having a good synchronicity between work and life won't make up for it.

I am at a point in life where working toward my FUTURE SUCCESS motive, my big ambitions, is taking a considerable amount of my time. When people have asked what I'm doing for the weekend and I respond with "writing my book," I get messages like "hell yeah!" and "you got this," but I also hear criticism: "This book is taking too much of your time" and "You shouldn't work so much." At times when people have said these things or implied I'm doing something wrong by making work a priority, it's made me feel crappy at first. But then I remember that the impact I'm making with my work makes me happy, and my biggest goals right now are work goals rather than nonwork goals. That is where more of my time and energy naturally flow because I want it that way. I get to wake up and have a real chance to pursue my dream. Not everyone can say they have that opportunity; it's hard work but work I am grateful for. I remind myself that we are all different and our seasons of life can change. I remember that years ago I had many personal goals I focused on, and had more free time to spend on travel, relationships, climbing mountains, and other things, but now I am in a different season of life.

The need to have a life outside of work is still important to me, and I make a concerted effort to notice if I am neglecting my personal life. In the future, the need to tip the scale toward personal time and goals may be at the forefront for my well-being, but currently maximizing my "balance" between the two isn't what should drive my decision-making for my optimal work life.

HAVING LESS IMPORTANT MOTIVES MET ISN'T ENOUGH

If a motive isn't as strong as you might like it to be, but it's not one of your most dominant needs, it most likely won't be detrimental and, in fact, you can still be incredibly happy at work. Here's a case in point. PERSONAL STRENGTHS, PEER APPRECIATION, and COMPANY APPRECIATION aren't particularly strong for me in my current work situation, yet I have high well-being. (In chapter 8 I will show you how you can evaluate your well-being.)

What's also true is that when many motives are thriving for you but none of them are in your top 5, it's not enough. If, for example, PERSONAL STRENGTHS, PEER APPRECIATION, and COMPANY APPRECIATION were highly met needs but my most important needs weren't doing so hot, my quality of work life would plummet. Likewise, if many of the 28 motives are strong for you but the needs that matter most are weak, then your quality of work life will suffer.

TAKEAWAY #3: EMBRACE THE DIVERSITY OF NEEDS

We were working with an HR manager to distribute the assessment and do a workshop with her company when I asked her what her top 5 motives were after she took the assessment. She told me her five motives and asked, "Are those good ones?" I replied there are no "good" or "bad" ones—no "right" answers. **Given we have varying degrees of need across the 28 motives, we must welcome motive diversity.** You must respect and embrace others' top motives just the way you want yours to be respected. But do we always do this? We sure don't!

I will get more into the nuances around motive diversity later in the book, but I want you to grasp this concept from the beginning. Certain motives can be idealized in our own minds or culture; some might be treated with favoritism in your workplace or take turns as buzzwords in society—such as AUTONOMY, BELONGING, PURPOSE, or INNOVATION. Meanwhile, other motives can be overlooked, judged, or misunderstood. FUN can be thought of as

frivolous; the need for CALMNESS, a weakness; having a BAL-
ANCED PACE, a luxury; COMPANY APPRECIATION might
be seen as unnecessary. In one organizational culture FAIRNESS
can be an important value, while at another company it's disre-
garded. One team may prioritize PEER APPRECIATION, while
for another team it's nonexistent.

PURPOSE is a good example for me to use here. It, like other
motives, can both be put on a pedestal by some and dismissed by
others. At times, there is a bias in favor of PURPOSE, yet some
people truly don't care about PURPOSE at work. Yep, I said it. Now
I know I might piss some people off who refer to motives like PAS-
SION and PURPOSE as the holy grail. I've gotten a side-eye from
people when I have said things like, "Actually, not everyone needs
a high level of AUTONOMY or BELONGING or WORK-LIFE
HARMONY or PURPOSE to be most fulfilled at work."

Recently I watched a webinar given by the head of people and
culture from a respected organization. The message was this: If you
want to retain people and keep them happy, the number one thing
you must do is cultivate a deeper meaning in employees' work.

I found that interesting. I had a friend who just quit a job where
she felt she truly was living her PURPOSE. She was a health and
fitness manager at a top fitness brand in New York that had blown
up on social media, her work was incredibly purpose-driven and she
was reaching so many people, she was doing the work she felt she was
meant to do, but having meaning in her job wasn't enough for her
because her other motives weren't met.

PURPOSE isn't the magical answer, and it doesn't help us to
position it or any other motive as such. Jessica, a digital marketer
at a software company, shared with me that she doesn't find much

meaning or purpose in her work, nor is she full of passion and love for what she does. She said, "My job is just a job, and I am more than fine with that! I do my job really well, I like achieving results and being looked up to as an expert in what I do, but to me my work is not something I am strongly passionate about." Jessica shared that she finds her life meaningful, PASSION and PURPOSE are manifested outside of work, and she is grateful that her work life doesn't get in the way of that. Her other motives—SECURITY, FLEXIBILITY, AUTONOMY, PERSONAL STRENGTHS, and ACHIEVEMENT—are strong, and she has the freedom, comfort, and satisfaction at work that support deeper meaning in her personal life.

Conversely, a woman shared with me her struggle in that she had been taught to view PURPOSE as lavish. Being raised as a first-generation immigrant, she felt her parents' values were very much focused on success in a corporate career, being practical and not a "hopeless dreamer," as they called it. But pursuing her love of writing in her career, the work she found most meaningful, was imperative for her to have her best work life. I've also heard stories on the opposite end of the spectrum, from people frustrated in their quest to find their PURPOSE because they were taught and made to believe from an early age in their family this is what they should do. One person shared he found himself finally happy in his career when the pressure for some grand PURPOSE was finally off the table for him.

The point is, no motive or mix of motives is necessarily the golden ticket; we shouldn't treat them as such or, on the opposite end of the spectrum, dismiss them. For you, whether finding meaning in helping customers solve problems or feeling your work is a bigger calling to what you are meant to do in life, PURPOSE may be a main influence on your well-being, while for others it's not. On the leader and organizational side, it's absolutely important for a leader to care about meeting the need for meaningful work, but it's just as important for them to care about meeting other needs that may be less glamorized or that they may not have been paying attention to.

You may be like me where my need for FUTURE SUCCESS is more important than WORK-LIFE HARMONY. You could have both of those motives in your top 5 and will have a more difficult time determining your action plan to meet both well, given they are on opposite ends of the Motives Circumplex, tougher to satisfy simultaneously. Or you could need WORK-LIFE HARMONY to thrive and not at all care about FUTURE SUCCESS. Maybe you do not have any future goals driving your well-being; you are content. In a society where we constantly hear the message that we should strive for more, a lack of need to achieve or grow—being contented—can be perceived as lack of drive and lead to judgment. Yet contentment is a vital aspect of personal growth itself and satisfaction. I respect that others I work with may be content and not striving toward a future goal or that they may need to harmonize more than I. We are all "right"; none of our motives are better than another.

TAKEAWAY #4: PEOPLE CAN STRUGGLE WITH, NEED, AND MEET THE SAME MOTIVES IN DIFFERENT WAYS

Even if two people have the same motive or a person has the same motive at different points in their work life, how that need gets met, why it's of top importance, and the obstacles to meeting it will be different.

- When it comes to having WORK-LIFE HARMONY, some people are separators, meaning they need clean boundaries between work time and personal time, a "start" and "stop" time. Others are integrators; they like an ebb and flow with flexibility. They might start working at six a.m., then take a break around noon to run errands or work out. They might stop working at three p.m. to be at their kid's game and then hop back on to work at eight p.m. Being able to bring their dog to work, working over a weekend so they can put in a three-day workweek—these are the kinds of things that appeal to integrators.

- You could struggle with ACHIEVEMENT because you put a lot of pressure on yourself to be perfect, are full of self-doubt, or never stop to recognize your success. A different person could struggle because they feel aimless or aren't the best about setting and working toward goals.

- A PRESTIGE-driven person may satisfy this motive by working for a startup with a mission they find admirable, while another person's value in PRESTIGE could mean working at a well-established company that has a brand name that is widely known and trusted.

- The desire for BELONGING may be important for one person because they have been bullied and discriminated against in a previous job because they are part of the LGBTQ+ community. They want to work somewhere where they are not only treated fairly but are truly welcomed. For another, BELONGING may be vital because it's part of the Peer Connection Domain and they are naturally a people person who is happiest when their social well-being is nurtured; they find a supportive, inclusive community to be deeply motivating.

- Having FUN at work to a younger version of you could have meant social outings and company perks. To the you today, FUN could be manifested through less stressful deadlines, and time to work on creative bigger-picture projects and to attend brainstorming sessions around new, innovative ideas.

- You could find TRUSTWORTHY LEADERSHIP to be important because you are a leader yourself, and being trusted and respected by your team is imperative to your work satisfaction, along with working alongside other leaders you find trustworthy. For someone else, the need to trust leadership could come from a painful history of working for bad leaders who lacked transparency, compassion, and honesty.

There is so much to learn about one another and ourselves when we reflect on and talk about motives. We can't assume our version of FUN is someone else's. We may not struggle with our need for SECURITY in the same way as another. Why motives are important, what they mean to you, how they get met, and the roadblocks to meeting them will vary from person to person.

TAKEAWAY #5: OUR MOTIVES WILL EVOLVE

The needs that are influencing your health and happiness most at work will change over time. Think about your younger self. Wouldn't you say your needs have changed both personally and professionally? Motives don't change rapidly from one day to the next, but some of them will shift over time. You start a new job, switch careers, experience what you consider to be a big failure, have a kid, go through a massive layoff, or become a manager—all these can influence your needs.

For example . . .

- You start a new job at a new organization, and to be successful you find CLEAR EXPECTATIONS to be an important part of navigating this new career journey.

- You finally take the leap and start your own company but are hungering to feel SECURITY and CALMNESS as you navigate entrepreneurial fears.

- You become a single dad and your need for FLEXIBILITY is more important than it ever was.

- You have been at the same company in similar roles for many years and are bored to death with the need to CHALLENGE yourself and have VARIETY.

- The younger you may have found GROWTH and INNO-VATION to be top work happiness drivers. Years later in your career you may find motives on the opposite side of the circumplex that are more relationship driven, such as PEER CONNECTION and PEER APPRECIATION, to be more important.

The motives that are deeply value-based and rooted in your belief system may not vary quite as much over the course of your career, but as life changes, motives can change with it.

THE UGLY TRUTH, THE TRUTH THAT SETS US FREE

The ugly truth is that well-being is messy, multifaceted, changing, and personal. I call it the ugly truth because as humans we don't like messy things; we would prefer to tie up well-being in a neat little bow with a perfect formula. There isn't a "destination" we arrive at where we are thriving or our employees are thriving and it stays that way. Rather, workplace well-being is constantly evolving. There isn't a straight and narrow path to follow to create a fulfilling work life or workplace with strong mental, emotional, and social health.

The formula isn't as simple as finding work I'm passionate about or working for a great boss equals fulfillment in my career. If I create a company culture with strong values, then people will want to stay. If I infuse gratitude and recognition in my team, then we'll collaborate better. There needs to be a shift from thinking there is one optimal approach or a one-size-fits-all approach to allowing for more individualized consideration. There are certainly broader best practices, tips, and actions for each motive. For example, if you have the BALANCED PACE motive, you must have systems in place to protect your time. Or if you want people to have AUTONOMY on your team, don't micromanage! But well-being needs to be as personalized as possible. It's about knowing—knowing yourself, knowing the people you work with, and knowing the people you lead on a human level.

When working with leaders around this new understanding to create their best workplace, I have seen reactions that spanned from sighs of relief and inspired ear-to-ear grins to trepidation and fear. Sometimes I see a bit of both, a mix of excitement along with an oh-crap-what-have-I-gotten-myself-into. Having this clarity, this path forward is reassuring, but it can also feel demanding. You have work to do! Results to achieve! Goals to meet! Yet this is the truth, whether you like it or not. Whether you embrace workplace well-being with open arms or reluctant acceptance, you are ultimately in a much more powerful position and can get the support you need because culture is on everyone, not just you. Trust me, as we stroll down this path together you will see how this is a more effective way, with big rewards.

PUTTING INSIGHTS INTO ACTION
DISCOVER YOUR UNIQUE MOTIVES

Now that you understand what a work life well-lived really means, it's time to put those insights into action and take the Motives Met Human Needs Assessment™ to uncover your motives, if you haven't already.

You can scan the QR code below on your phone or go to motivesmet.com/code to get your code and have it available for when you want to take the assessment. The survey will take you approximately fifteen minutes to complete.

Once the assessment is completed, you automatically receive your personal Motives Met Report. I will walk you through the different parts of your report as we travel the remainder of the pathway.

CHAPTER 4

WHY MOTIVES MATTER

Before we move on to the next part of the Motives Met Pathway and start to really dive into your motives, let's take a pit stop and further our understanding by talking about the backbone of all of this—the "why." We don't want to just go through the motions; we want to solidify deep in our bones why this matters so much, why you are doing what you are doing.

In 2023 we launched another study of 2,400 employees to further explore desired outcomes at work such as happiness, retention, less stress, and psychological safety—some areas we had already studied and some new ones. In this research we would determine differences between those with suffering work needs versus thriving ones. Respondents took our Motives Met Human Needs Assessment™, which identified their top 5 motives. They then told us how well each of these motives was being met in their current job. Based on their answers, we segmented them into three groups and saw a consistent decline across desired outcomes. Those with well-met motives made up 16% of the sample, those with moderately met motives measured 48%, and those with unmet motives comprised 36% of the sample.

THE RESEARCH SEGMENTS

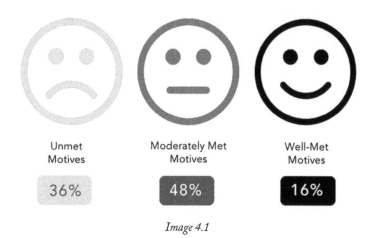

Image 4.1

I'm not going to pile on boring facts or go too in-depth on the research, but as I reveal different parts of why motives matter throughout this chapter, I'll share some of our data that supports it.

PEOPLE FIRST = NEEDS FIRST

"Having needs is not evidence of weakness—it is human."

—Danielle Bernock

Human beings are emotional beings, with needs and desires, yet this unavoidable truth is one most of us have been conditioned to think we can or should somehow escape when we go to work—whether that's a physical workplace or on virtual video meetings—or that there is an "off" button we can hit that shuts down our emotions and makes us dehumanized robots where our human needs disappear. This isn't possible, and this is Dream Killer #5.

Dream Killer #5:
We don't bring our humanity to work.

Hell, at one point I was so out of touch I didn't believe I deserved to have my human needs met at work until I had made it, until I had suffered enough to earn it. It's quite sad that we are conditioned to believe we have to earn the right to be human! My belief was subconscious, but I can look back now and see how I had been taught professionalism equals dehumanization.

Brené Brown, author of *Dare to Lead* and pioneer of research on vulnerability, calls this "armoring up"—to be professional, to protect ourselves and avoid being vulnerable. We bury our emotions, fake how we feel, and wear our workplace armor. This can manifest as pressuring ourselves to be perfect, never wanting to break a sweat and admit we're stressed, avoiding important conversations so as to not rock the boat, not being able to express negative emotions, not going after important goals, and not taking worthwhile risks. This armor doesn't help us in the long run, as we tend to underestimate the emotional needs we inevitably carry with us at work—not to mention that our emotions will spill out in unhealthy ways if suppressed.

Author Leah Weiss hits on this perfectly in her book *How We Work*. She says, "Nothing provides more opportunities than the workplace for us to feel discouraged, disappointed, bored, overwhelmed, envious, embarrassed, anxious, irritated, outraged, and afraid to say what we really feel. Like it or not, aware of it or not, we feel things at our jobs, and how we feel at and about work matters—to us, to our families and friends who are impacted, to the quality of our work, and ultimately to the success of the organizations we work for."[1]

Ignoring our emotions is to ignore a significant part of being human, and it also puts our values at risk. If we want environments and relationships that uplift health and happiness at work, how can that happen if we tend to show up as lesser versions of ourselves? The virtues we value and try to exemplify in our personal life, such as compassion, trust, acceptance, kindness, and respect, are less likely to shine through when blocked by our protective armor at work. As I reflect back, I can see how true this was of myself. I felt I couldn't show weakness, so I had little patience or compassion when others showed weaknesses and imperfection. I thought you should just be tough and deal with the stress or frustration, so I showed less kindness when others struggled.

In recent years, more of the world has caught on to the idea that we need work to be more human-centric and we should take off some of our workplace armor if we want to take well-being seriously.

A "people-first" work culture has become an almost catchy marketing phrase that is thrown around yet still often feels void of clarity of what a more human experience at work means.

Prioritizing people means prioritizing our human needs and the emotions fueling those needs.

To be well, we can't suppress our needs and feelings at work, but caring for them can also be tricky. Expecting all of our needs to be met all the time isn't realistic, nor is it healthy to shift from emotional suppression to the opposite end of the spectrum, what I think of as emotional vomiting—expressing feelings of anger, stress, fear, or annoyance as often as we like, with no regard for others.

Venting emotions without boundaries can also be harmful to the well-being of people in HR and leadership. While organizations are understanding the necessity to care for the mental, emotional, and social health of their employees, leaders and managers are also not therapists. They should be supportive allies and coaches but not mental health professionals or emotional punching bags.

WHICH "SELF" SHOULD WE BRING TO WORK?

The expression "bring your whole self to work" has gained traction in recent years. Mike Robbins, author of *Bring Your Whole Self to Work: How Vulnerability Unlocks Creativity, Connection, and Performance*, says "For us to truly succeed, especially in today's business world, we must be willing to bring our *whole selves* to the work that we do. And for the teams and organizations that we're a part of to thrive, it's also essential to create an environment where people feel safe enough to bring all of who they are to work."[2]

But is it truly safe to bring your "whole self" to work? Do you want other people to do this? Some believe the idea of the "whole self" at work is taking it too far, that we shouldn't show up as completely unfiltered versions of ourselves.

We have entered an era where people are trying to figure out how best to be human and to keep our feelings in the workplace within the right boundaries. If you are operating under the mindset that your "work self" and your "human self" must be vastly different, not only will your well-being suffer, but chances are you might not be embracing or respecting others' humanity. Creating a more human work experience sounds lovely in theory, but how do we do that well? How do we make sure we don't go from emotional suppression all the way to emotional vomiting? Where we don't feel we need to be our "fake selves" but also maybe not our "whole selves" that include our "worst selves."

MOTIVES HELP US BRING OUR HUMAN SELVES TO WORK

Having our human needs met comes down to how we want to feel at work. When motives are met, we feel more of the human emotions we want to feel, and when they are undermet, we feel more of the human emotions we do not want to feel. The ability to be more aware and welcoming of motives allows us to embrace our humanity at work in a productive way; it helps with both EIs—emotional intelligence and emotional inclusion.

The better you are at identifying and being consciously aware of the motives that profoundly influence our emotional state as humans, the more likely you are to make wise decisions and take strategic actions that benefit you and the people around you. Dan Goleman, author of *Emotional Intelligence*, states that emotional intelligence gives us the ability to recognize, understand, and manage our own emotions as well as recognize, understand, and influence the emotions of others. The emotions we feel every day compel us to take action and influence our decisions in profound ways.

Goleman says, "The word 'motivation' shares its root with 'emotion': both come from the Latin *motere*, to move. Our motives give us our aims and the drive to achieve them."[3] When your motives are well met, your emotional experience motivates you in a positive direction.

When we embrace motive diversity, we are creating emotional inclusion at work, we are saying all of these needs and their intertwined emotions are justified and welcome. Ludmila Praslova, PhD, refers to emotional inclusion as things like normalizing emotional truthfulness and honest answers, not judging emotions and checking our cultural and personal biases. Emotional inclusion helps combat toxic positivity, which takes an emotional toll on many at work. Toxic positivity is the belief that even if you are feeling less desired emotions, you should have a positive mindset, deny your true feelings, and exhibit "good vibes only." She writes, "It robs us of authenticity. It guilts and shames us when we need support. Toxic positivity does not create true optimism, it creates denial and distortion. And denial and distortion prevent us from truly dealing with and addressing our situations."[4] If needs are suffering, then we need to be able to talk about why. Emotional openness in a work culture encourages people to be human.

If we want to be mentally healthy humans at work, then we need to embrace being human—with needs, struggles, mistakes, and the feelings behind them, and we need to embrace the humanness of others. We need to be able to express that we are afraid to fail. We need to be allowed to say we are angry because someone treated us unjustly. We need to be able to voice if we feel too stressed or undervalued. This is also true for leaders and managers, as often they can feel immense pressure to be perfect rather than human.

MEETING MOTIVES WILL AMPLIFY DESIRABLE EXPERIENCES

Every motive is connected to core desired feelings and emotional experiences we want to feel more of at work. When the PRESTIGE motive is strong, you will feel pride for the work you do at your organization. When the need for SECURITY is met, you will feel safe. When you have BELONGING, you will feel accepted.

Likewise, when motives are weak, you are more likely to have a less desirable emotional experience. When the VARIETY motive is weak, you may feel bored. When the need for ACHIEVEMENT isn't met, you may feel shame. When you don't have PASSION, you may feel indifferent.

I am purposeful in not labeling these "positive" or "good" emotions versus "negative" or "bad" because while we generally want to feel less of certain things at work, they're part of our natural human experience. In fact, they can be useful. They can send us important messages if we pay attention to them. Stress can be a sign you care about your work; fear can be an indication that you're taking an exciting risk that helps meet your INNOVATION or ACHIEVEMENT motive. The goal is managing these emotions well, not entirely eliminating stress or fear. Of course, if we find we are continuously anxious, bored, afraid, or annoyed at work, that signals that a motive is suffering and needs improvement.

Image 4.2 shows that when your motives are met, you are much more likely to have the desired emotions and experiences you seek in your work life. For example, 74% of people with well-met motives are frequently happy at work compared to only 32% with unmet motives. And 71% of those with well-met motives feel motivated at work compared to 29% with unmet motives.

To What Extent Do You Feel the Following Currently in Your Job?

Frequently

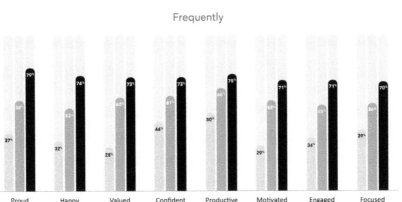

Image 4.2

THE ROOT CAUSE OF WORK STRESS IS UNMET MOTIVES

Ah, stress. Stress and work seem to go hand in hand, don't they? As I mentioned earlier, in my coaching practice, work is always at the top of the list for my clients. Stress has become big business. The stress management industry is booming, but it tends to focus not on the root cause but on reducing the symptoms of stress, whether it's with CBD oils, breathing exercises, or advice on decreasing one's screen time.

Kelly McGonigal is a psychologist, author, and award-winning lecturer at Stanford University, and she hits the nail on the head when she says the "stress-reduction industry" operates a lot like the diet industry, "which sows seeds of dissatisfaction and offers a lot of quick fixes but doesn't always empower people to create sustainable change in their well-being."[5]

These are the types of things that fuel our Band-Aid dream killer. As we know, organizations are guilty of this, too. They can have a webinar that teaches ways to manage stress for their employees, which can be a nice thing to do. But the reality is if a worker is highly stressed because their needs aren't met—whether that's feeling safe at work, feeling their manager has their best interest at heart, or feeling their workload is manageable—that webinar will mean absolutely nothing and can actually make workers feel worse and more frustrated.

One of the definitions of stress I find incredibly useful in my work comes from my meditation teacher davidji. davidji is a global leader in the meditation world, an internationally recognized stress management expert, and the author of the book *Destressifying*. He is a teacher at Unplug Meditation who taught me when I became certified and has taught thousands of people in the military, law enforcement, and the corporate world how to transform their relationship with stress. He defines stress as how we respond when our needs are not met. Our top motives are the things we need most; when they are not met, our response is the stress that naturally follows. The more a motive suffers, the greater the stress that will ensue. Our research shows in Image 4.3 that those with unmet motives are much more stressed at work (47%) and those with well-met motives are significantly less stressed (18%).

As I previously emphasized, stress, along with other unwanted feelings like worry, doubt, frustration, and fear, are part of the human experience. We will never be rid of these emotions, and they serve important and even positive purposes in life whether we like it or not. It's not about expecting to have our needs met all the time so we never stress. We will always have unmet needs, but our important human needs at work should be healthy and thus our stress manageable.

How Frequently in the Last 6 Months Have You
Felt Stressed from Your Current Job?

Frequently

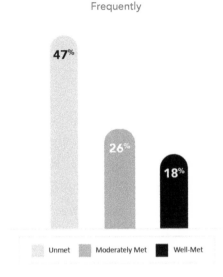

Image 4.3

Stress as unmet needs can look like this:

- Unmet FREE EXPRESSION motive—feeling you can't speak up with your opinion when you believe decisions that are being made at work are a mistake.

- Unmet TRUSTWORTHY LEADERSHIP motive—working with leaders who care most about numbers and getting work done at whatever human cost.

- Unmet PASSION motive—wanting to do work that excites and inspires you, but not knowing what your passion is and how to discover it.

- Unmet BALANCED PACE motive—being constantly rushed with tight timelines on important work, limiting your creativity and quality of output.

- Unmet INNOVATION motive—feeling like you can't flex your creative muscles and must conform to the status quo.

- Unmet ACHIEVEMENT motive—being driven to succeed but having a fixed rather than growth mindset and goals that are rigid and unattainable.

Psychologist Nick Wignall also makes the case that stress management techniques will only take you so far. There instead needs to be considerable focus on managing the stressors, which are your unmet motives. He says, "Stress management techniques like 5 minutes a day of mindfulness or a weekly massage are appealing because they're relatively low risk. But often they're just a distraction—a way to procrastinate on addressing the real issues in your life that are causing stress in the first place."[6]

When I was coaching clients on their stress and anxiety, I would always refer to stress as a blanket emotion because our true feelings like to hide beneath the covers. We have a tendency to generalize everything as stress, but the more I pulled back the covers with clients (and myself!) there was usually more to the story. Their "stress" was their fear that they didn't have what it took to leave their job and go freelance. Their "stress" was their anger at being given a poor review when the feedback was the first time they were hearing it. Their "stress" was feeling overwhelmed with work that was expected of them that they didn't have the full knowledge to accomplish.

It's become acceptable and common to say you are stressed, but admitting to others or yourself that you are fearful, angry, or overwhelmed can be more difficult. When important human needs are met at work, there is less stress. But if stress is running high, then embracing motives in your work life and workplace helps pinpoint the foundational stressor(s) at work and the feelings that stem from them. When you shift from stress management to stressor management, you then have more power to manage the stress by treating the root problem versus the symptoms.

MEETING MOTIVES PREVENTS PEOPLE FROM BURNING OUT

According to the APA Dictionary of Psychology, burnout is defined as "physical, emotional or mental exhaustion, accompanied by decreased motivation, lowered performance and negative attitudes toward oneself and others." Often burnout is associated with being overworked, having too many tasks without enough time to do them, and working yourself into a state where your flame burns out. But there are many reasons that burnout happens.

One study found five main factors that cause burnout, and they are all directly related to unmet motives:[7]

1. Unmanageable workload—WORK-LIFE HARMONY and CALMNESS motives

2. Unfair treatment at work—FAIRNESS motive

3. Lack of role clarity—CLEAR EXPECTATIONS motive

4. Lack of communication and support from manager— MANAGER SUPPORT and TRUSTWORTHY LEADERSHIP motives

5. Unreasonable time pressure—BALANCED PACE motive

Christina Maslach, creator of the Maslach Burnout Inventory and the pioneer of research on burnout, identified six main causes of burnout in her work. Two of them overlap with the five factors above, but other ones she found include:

- Poor relationships—BELONGING and PEER CONNECTION motives

- Lack of recognition—COMPANY APPRECIATION, PEER APPRECIATION and SELF-ESTEEM motives

- Perceived lack of control—AUTONOMY and FLEXIBILITY motives

- Mismatched values and skills—SHARED CULTURE motive

Another research study showed that people's unconscious needs can create burnout when their work does not meet those needs.[8] **When there is a mismatch between someone's needs and the opportunities and demands of the workplace, burnout happens.** Based on this finding, researchers suggested that one way to reduce burnout was to adjust the job environment to better meet their people's needs. Or as we like to put it, meet people's motives. As Image 4.4 shows, our research also validates that 40% of people with unmet needs are often burnt out at work, which is double those with well-met needs, at only 17%.

Stress is inevitable at work and in life, but burnout is not. To stop burnout from happening, similar to stress, we have to treat the root cause. Jennifer Moss, author of the book *The Burnout Epidemic*, says, "We tend to think of burnout as an individual problem, solvable by 'learning to say no,' more yoga, better breathing techniques,

How Frequently Do You Experience Burnout
From Your Current Job?

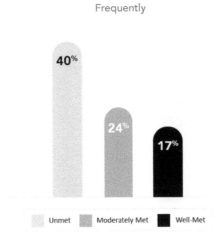

Image 4.4

practicing resilience—the self-help list goes on. But evidence is mounting that applying personal Band-Aid solutions to an epic and rapidly evolving workplace phenomenon may be harming, not helping, the battle."[9] Learning to say no is helpful, but burnout is not just a personal issue, it's a workplace culture problem.

MET MOTIVES = A BETTER WORK LIFE

"You don't have to earn the right to have a need."

—Kate Northrup

What this all comes down to is that when people have their top needs met, they feel they have greater mental health and well-being, and that they are living best work life. That is the ultimate goal.

To What Degree Are You Living Your Best Possible Work Life?

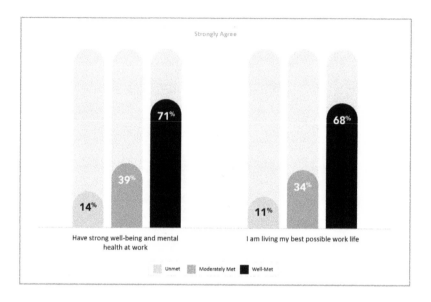

Image 4.5

Another reminder that if you want to dive into our research in greater depth, you can access our research report at motivesmet.com/research-and-approach.

CHAPTER 5

MOTIVES MATTER FOR ORGANIZATIONS

Well-being is not soft or insignificant. It shouldn't be secondary on an organization's agenda; it should be first because people should come first, and what people need is for their needs to come first. When you as a leader or company take care of your employees' needs, they will take care of yours—your strategic objectives, your customers, your tough problems. I have had many managers, HR leaders, culture consultants, and even employees ask me how to get their CEO, boss, or shareholders to understand the imperative of having happy and healthy employees in their workplace. My stomach drops every time because I can't believe how some people still don't get it. Perhaps numbers and impactful examples can help them understand. So all right, if they need evidence, we'll give it to them. Let's explore data and stories that bring to life why motives matter from the organizational lens.

NEED SATISFACTION = JOB SATISFACTION

"You don't build a business—you build people—and then people build the business."   **—Zig Ziglar**

When you create a culture where human needs are cared for, you attract and captivate high-quality people. Even though I sometimes still use the term "retention," as it's a commonly understood term, I prefer to use "captivate" instead. Retention feels transactional and inhuman to me, as it means the continued possession, use, or control of someone. Whereas to captivate is to attract and hold the interest and attention of someone, which is what organizations should strive to do.

> People-first means putting human needs first, and need satisfaction equates to job satisfaction.

This is a big deal because it's become more difficult and competitive to **attract and captivate** the best people. Your aim is to **captivate** people so they are engaged, motivated, and happy rather than quitting or "quiet quitting," which is a term that emerged post-pandemic to describe people who haven't physically left the building but are mentally checked out, disengaged, or doing the bare minimum and no more.

Companies can get tunnel vision on revenue numbers, but the reality is voluntary turnover is a pricey problem that will affect your bottom line in a big way.

- Losing an employee can cost a company 1.5–2 times the employee's salary.[1]
- On average, it costs a company six to nine months of an employee's salary to replace him or her.[2]
- C-suite turnover can cost 213% of salary.[3]
- The cost of voluntary turnover for businesses in the United States in 2022 was estimated at over one trillion dollars.[4]

When a role is vacant, along with the time needed to ramp up and transition new people once hired, the result is missed or delayed revenue. There is the time and dollars needed to recruit and teach new hires. There is the risk of greater mistakes, things falling through the cracks, and quality of service going down for clients or customers or even losing those relationships and the business that comes with them altogether. I saw that happen at that terrible company I worked at. We had lost three team members on the creative team and one account manager in a year, and the client was like, "What in the hell is going on over there?" They lost trust in the company. They were frustrated they no longer got to work with the people on our team they had a good relationship with and had lost an established way of working that made their life easier. So they left.

And maybe the worst of it all is that when many employees quit, it damages employee morale and culture. It makes people wonder, "If they are leaving for a better job with greater happiness, should I consider doing the same?" Research shows turnover breeds more turnover. It hurts even more when you lose people who are admired by many—an innovator, trusted leader, or top performer. People who leave create a void. Others are left to pick up the slack until a new person is hired and actually knows what the heck they are doing, which can take a considerable amount of time. Even if a role is "filled" within a few weeks, more often than not it's not really filled; it takes the new person time to be able to perform at the level the person leaving did. If a cohesive team works with one another well, the entire dynamic changes when a person leaves and a new one comes in. Then there is the organization's reputation—you get a bad rap if you are known for constantly losing people, which will prevent you from attracting the best people to work at your organization. When people leave, it rocks the entire boat.

The cycle is really quite nonsensical: Companies spend less money to captivate and then are stuck paying *more* money to attract and train new people. Want to know what's even more messed up? According to Gallup research, 52% of employees choosing to leave say their manager or organization could have done something to stop them from leaving. Fifty-one percent of employees leaving cited that in the three months before leaving, no manager or leader talked with them about their job satisfaction or future in the company.[5] The organization could have stopped people from leaving, but they didn't. They could have had a simple conversation, but they didn't.

In a Gallup article, *This Fixable Problem Costs U.S. Businesses $1 Trillion*, the authors say, "Here's how you plug a million-dollar leak in your company: Train your managers to have frequent, meaningful conversations with employees about what really matters to them. What's frustrating them? What are their dreams? Where do they want to go?"[6]

Leaders and supervisors need to have meaningful conversations with their people about their motives. In our own research we found that 33% of employees said their boss has never met with them to talk about their job satisfaction and needs that are driving or inhibiting their well-being at work in the past year; 31% said they have had such a conversation only once.

A whole step on our Motives Met Pathway, the *COMMUNI-CATE* step, is dedicated to this and is to come shortly. The point is, do everyone a favor and invest your money up front into meeting the needs of your people rather than draining your bank account with turnover costs. Employees with strong met motives are less likely to be looking elsewhere for a new job now: 80% with well-met motives intend to stay at their organization for the next year compared to only 41% with unmet motives. Those with strong motives also have greater intention to stay at their organization for the long-haul—67% with well-met motives and only 33% with unmet motives.

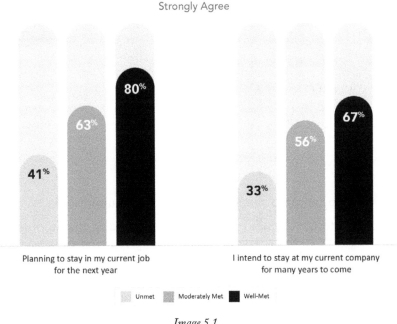

Image 5.1

MEETING MOTIVES GROWS COMPANY CONNECTION

I have heard so many incredible "motive stories" since we have started our company Motives Met, but let me share one with you that I feel beautifully shows the relationship between met motives and commitment and connection to an organization. Carlos is a sales account manager at a financial tech company. His motives are: TRUSTWORTHY LEADERSHIP, SHARED CULTURE, PRESTIGE, GROWTH, and FUTURE SUCCESS.

Image 5.2 Carlos's Motives Circumplex

An important step along the Motives Met Pathway is to evaluate the degree to which each of your top needs is being met in order to diagnose how healthy they are. We will talk more about evaluating motives on this step, to determine if motives are drowning, suffering, coasting, or thriving. This is how Carlos rated the health of his motives.

- TRUSTWORTHY LEADERSHIP—thriving

- SHARED CULTURE—thriving

- PRESTIGE—coasting

- GROWTH—thriving

- FUTURE SUCCESS—coasting

Carlos's motives are looking pretty dang good. All of his top needs are in the upper-right quadrant of the Motives Circumplex, all in the Company Connection and Advancement Domain. Now, how long has he been at his company? Twelve years. He has been consistently promoted, adding great value and profit to the business, and his intent is to stay for the longer haul. He is working toward a C-suite leadership position in the company. Why? He loves it there. His needs are well cared for.

Later in the book I'll share more of his story, which is an inspiring one. But Carlos is one powerful example of many that shows those who don't believe that prioritizing well-being in their organizations and taking care of their people is good for business. There is abundant proof that if you put people first, profits will follow, that they are mutually enhancing, and that good things will happen—more innovation, greater loyalty, and increased collaboration.

> People who have their motives met are more likely to believe you care, and caring goes both ways: When employees feel cared for, they care more about their company.

Image 5.3 shows employees with well-met motives score significantly higher on feeling their company cares about their well-being (78% for well-met motives and only 20% for unmet). They in turn care about their company's well-being (78% for well-met motives and only 43% for unmet) and are committed to the company and its goals (77% for well-met motives and only 39% for unmet). They also believe the peers at their company care about one another's well-being and are much more likely to recommend their friends work at their company.

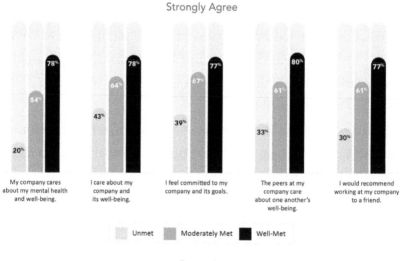

Image 5.3

If you are a leader, you might be thinking that of course your employees know you care, but leaders also tend to believe they are perceived differently than they are. A study by Deloitte showed that just 56% of workers feel that their company's executive leaders care about their well-being, but a whopping 91% of the C-suite think that they are perceived as caring about it.[7] Talk about a misalignment!

While being treated like a number, not a human, at work was never something people were okay with, it has always been something they felt they had to put up with. But today the tides have turned and people expect their employers to care about their workers' well-being. And caring matters. Research has shown that teams who feel their company cares about their well-being achieve higher profitability, greater productivity, and increased customer engagement.

FOSTERING PSYCHOLOGICAL SAFETY AND TRUST

To have a team or organization where motives are strong, people need to talk about them, which will include uncomfortable conversations. A motive conversation could be related to why you don't feel you're getting the guidance you need from your manager (MANAGER SUPPORT motive), that, as the new or junior person on the team, your opinions are not taken into consideration (SELF-ESTEEM motive), that you feel you need additional learning opportunities to keep up with the competition your team is up against in your industry (GROWTH motive), or that you don't feel it will be possible to reach your goals if you follow this path (ACHIEVEMENT motive). That means people must have psychological safety and trust to speak about these things honestly, otherwise it won't happen.

The "official" definition of psychological safety as pioneered by Amy Edmundson, organizational behavioral scientist and Harvard professor who brought the idea to the masses, is "the belief that one will not be punished or humiliated for speaking up with ideas, questions, concerns, or mistakes, and that the team is safe for interpersonal risk taking."[8] Essentially that means psychological safety is a group dynamic where people confidently feel they can honestly communicate, be vulnerable, bring up uncomfortable truths, and generally be themselves without fear or worry. The FREE EXPRESSION motive is closely tied with psychological safety, as people with a strong affinity for FREE EXPRESSION thrive in professional dynamics that are open, welcome authentic communication, and where psychological safety is strong.

Psychological safety and trust are closely intertwined, but psychological safety is a group phenomenon. For example, if I reveal the real me, ask this question, say what I need or something I disagree with, how will that be received by my team/this group (psychological safety) versus how will that be received by this person (trust)? Psychological safety gained further attention after Amy Edmundson brought it to light through Google's project Aristotle. In 2012 Google went on a quest to determine what factors set their highest-performing teams apart from other teams. They uncovered that having psychological safety was the *most* important factor. The problem is, as Amy Edmundson says, it's missing in most workplaces. People believe there will be consequences if they speak up. They don't feel they can bring their "human" to work, one of our dream killers. People naturally try to avoid conflict.

Good communication is a huge part of meeting motives, and psychological safety, along with trust, are key ingredients to that communication being effective. Given this, it's no surprise that people whose motives are met also feel stronger degrees of psychological safety and trust. In image 5.4 you can see that 78% of employees with highly met motives trust the people they work with, compared to only 35% with unmet motives. Important aspects of psychological safety such as "I feel comfortable being my true self at work" are much stronger for those with well-met motives (75%), and low for people with unmet motives (39%).

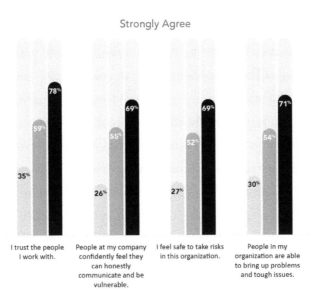

Strongly Agree

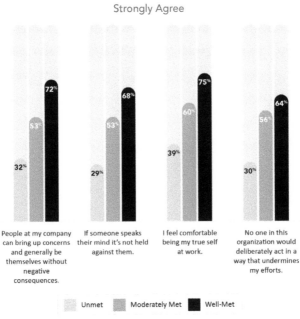

Strongly Agree

Image 5.4

When you bring motives into the heart of your organization, you aren't implementing a one-off-program. You aren't using fake Band-Aid fixes. You aren't simply talking about a people-first culture, you are living it. You are showing you care, that well-being matters, that your employees as humans matter. That doesn't mean you won't run into limitations. There may be motives your organization is naturally weak in due to the nature of your business, and others it is especially strong in. It's important to be honest about your weak areas, do what is possible to strengthen them, or compensate in other motive areas where possible. As a manager, you may not have the power to make some of the changes you would like for a person or your team. Employees know their supervisor or HR manager doesn't have the authority to change everything in the organization, but feeling seen, understood, and that you want to take action where possible and offer your support where you are able, matters in a big way.

Now that our *UNDERSTAND* step is complete and we have laid out all the benefits that come with met motives, it's time to move to the next step on the pathway: to *BE MINDFUL* of motives.

BE MINDFUL

UNDERSTAND · BE MINDFUL · EVALUATE · COMMUNICATE · MEET MOTIVES

CHAPTER 6

BECOMING MINDFUL TO MEET YOUR MOTIVES

The second step down the Motives Met Pathway is to *BE MINDFUL* of motives—taking a conscious, purposeful approach to keeping motives healthy for ourselves and others, which can be a struggle. I invited you to take the Motives Met Human Needs Assessment™ at the end of chapter 3, but if you haven't taken it yet, now would be a good time to pause and complete it, as this is where we start to really dive into your personal top 5 motives, which you will discover after taking the assessment. Instructions to obtain your code are on page 301.

It wasn't until I started studying mindfulness that I realized how much we sleepwalk through our lives, that our tendency is to operate on autopilot, going through the motions, hurrying through the day, doing the same things the same way, having life happen to us instead of intentionally creating our life. In many areas of life, including work and our work relationships, we can take a backseat approach, be inclined to tolerate what is, and wait for things to just change or get better. Dream Killer #6 is we take a passive or reactive approach to caring for health and happiness at work, not a preventive and proactive one.

Dream Killer #6:

We take a passive or reactive approach to caring for health and happiness at work, not a preventive and proactive one.

As I talked with people about their thoughts and feelings on work well-being and job satisfaction, I asked questions like:

- "What are you doing to support your health and happiness at work?"

- "How are you creating a positive emotional experience at your company?"

- "What steps do you take to create a people-first culture?"

- "What are you doing to manage your stressors at work or on your team?"

Many times I was met with a blank stare or a spewed-out answer related to something like not checking emails at night or taking lunch breaks. I would hear about working from home or working toward goals. I would hear from leaders about unlimited PTO for their people or a mental health program. Not that these things can't be helpful, but these answers were sometimes more haphazard than purposeful. Some people were able to provide deliberate answers, but many had to give the questions a lot of thought and still seemed to struggle to answer in a way they felt satisfied or confident about. In a similar fashion to how people responded to how to define well-being at work, clearly well-being wasn't often top of mind, people were going through the motions day in and day out, and they were more guessing than confident around how to truly create their best work lives and workplaces.

What I noticed when I asked people these questions was that I would sometimes hear more complaints than solutions: How stressed they are. How underappreciated they feel. How their team isn't working well together. How lost they are. How awful their boss or coworker is. How employees are stressed and disengaged. How they don't want to be in their career anymore. How they aren't qualified for the job they want. I would hear more about the problems and less about their strategy to avoid, fix, or solve these problems.

Mindfulness has been defined in many ways, but one simple yet powerful perspective for me has been that **to live a mindful life is to live life on purpose, with purpose**. When mindful, we shift from passive or reactive mode to being proactive and preventive with our well-being. We shift from judgment and control to compassion and acceptance. From being unaware of our needs and emotions to being consciously aware. From being thoughtless in our actions and interactions with others to being thoughtful.

MOTIVE MINDFULNESS EMPOWERS US TO BE PROACTIVE

Aristotle said, "Knowing yourself is the beginning of all wisdom." But knowing and accurately examining ourselves isn't all that easy.

We now know to live your best work life you must get your most important needs met, but we don't always know what we need most. We have blind spots and don't always allow ourselves to embrace those human needs and emotions, let alone be mindful of them. That's why we wanted to create our assessment: to help people become aware and more intentional with their human work needs and the five motives they personally need to be most mindful of. The Human Needs Assessment gives people the gift of mindfulness, which is a catalyst for growth, positive change, and gratitude. I want to emphasize gratitude here. It isn't all about what's going wrong or needs to change, but also noticing, celebrating, and safeguarding what's going well.

When you are not mindful of the motives that are the most influential to your well-being, you can pay the price. My friend Heather is a great example. She is a manager at a health-care company, and last year she was offered a new job within her organization. It was technically a step down in job title (though it wouldn't affect her salary), but she would be transitioning to the coveted brand side of the business. She was flattered they wanted to offer her the position, but she almost turned it down. Actually, she did at first turn it down. Why? She felt content, secure, and comfy with where she was. She had good work-life balance, friends she enjoyed working with, and a boss she trusted and liked. But after she took the Motives Met Human Needs Assessment™, she could see she was making a big decision based on outdated, less important needs.

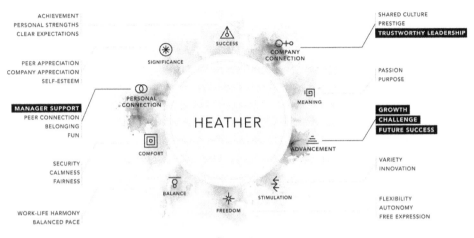

Image 6.1

Here's what Heather said about her choices.

I wasn't necessarily expecting advancement to be of great importance for my happiness at work, but I got all three motives in the Advancement Domain, CHALLENGE, GROWTH, and FUTURE SUCCESS. I knew I wanted to advance in my career, but I didn't realize that I was at the place where I was really ready for it and that I truly wanted to have an even bigger leadership role one day. The information in my Motives Met Report helped me to think through all of this. For example when I reviewed the questions around my CHALLENGE motive, I could see it was weak. I couldn't remember the last time I felt inspired to push myself at work, and I was becoming bored and under-challenged in my role.

When thinking about this job opportunity through the lens of my FUTURE SUCCESS motive, I knew this new job was it. If I stayed in my current role there was some limited room for growth, but it would be within a smaller side of our business. The potential long term wouldn't be as great as if I took the new position on the brand side of things, which is the core of our business and would put me on a bigger path with more potential.

Staying on my current default path wouldn't strengthen my needs in the way that taking the new position would. It was uncomfortable to think about the unknown. I wasn't thrilled at the thought of needing to build new relationships, and I would need, in the beginning at least, to put in more hours to get up to speed. But I could see that this is what I needed to do to get what I truly wanted. Plus, I am in a different phase than I was a few years ago. My youngest son is now three, I have childcare figured out, I could afford to put in some extra hours that I couldn't have afforded before.

My other two motives, MANAGER SUPPORT and TRUST-WORTHY LEADERSHIP, were strong in my current position. Knowing these motives are important to me, I made sure to ask around and see what I could find out about the reputation of leadership on the team I would be joining. I asked good questions of my new boss to get a sense of his management style and if we would work well together.

THE THREE A's OF A MINDFUL APPROACH TO WORK WELLNESS

Being mindful of motives requires what I call the three A's: conscious *awareness*, focused *attention*, and intentional *action*. Heather's story shows the power of the three A's in action. Let's talk about each in greater detail.

CONSCIOUS AWARENESS

"Awareness is the greatest agent for change."   **—Eckhart Tolle**

The first place you have to start is gaining conscious awareness of your motives. I use the word "conscious" because being consciously aware of your needs is having a heightened sense of awareness, which is different from just vaguely knowing in the back of your mind that a motive like MANAGER SUPPORT, FLEXIBILITY, or VARIETY is important. With the assessment, a spotlight shines on the things that matter so these needs can be at the forefront of your mind.

Knowing what we truly need can be half the battle. Seth J. Gillihan, PhD, a psychologist specializing in mindfulness-centered cognitive behavioral therapy, says, **"Knowing our needs doesn't guarantee that they'll be met, but it does raise the odds in our favor. Then we can focus on the important work of honoring our needs in the same way that we would honor those of the people we care about."**[1] Awareness is power. And part of that power is not in just knowing what you need most, but why you need it most. It helps you understand yourself on a deeper, more meaningful level. In Heather's story you can see upgrading her work life for the better started with the newfound awareness of her motives. With that awareness she was then able to reflect on why those needs mattered to her in this present moment of her work life.

FOCUSED ATTENTION

"If you continually ask yourself, 'What's important now,' then you won't waste time on the trivial."   **—Lou Holtz**

Mindfulness, in its most basic terms, is the intentional use of attention. The most important thing in your life isn't time, but your attention, which is your greatest asset. What you give your attention to will influence how your life unfolds. Each day there are so many things vying for your precious attention, and this includes your needs and desires. With only so many resources, hours, dollars, and commitments you can make, where do you focus? Rather than spread yourself thin and fragment that precious attention, you can focus on nurturing the motives that matter most. As Jim Collins, author of the book *Good to Great: Why Some Companies Make the Leap . . . and Others Don't*, says, "If you have more than three priorities you have none."[2] Sorry, Jim, we cheated: We have five. But you get the idea: You need to streamline your focus and resources, and if you have too many priorities, you essentially have none.

In an ideal world for you, maybe eighteen out of 28 motives would be flourishing. But using eighteen motives as a compass for how to get to your greatest health and happiness at work isn't a good strategy. **Trying to get everywhere will get you nowhere.** And it's not incredibly realistic. Given some motives can be tough to satisfy well at the same time, it can be difficult to get your top 5 in sync, let alone 28. What I appreciate about our approach is that it's ambitious yet realistic; things won't be perfect. I'll say that again, things *will not* be perfect, but if you can get your top 5 motives healthy, then your work life will be healthy, too.

Take Heather, for example. If she wasn't focused on her five core motives first, she would have made a poor decision and not taken the new job. It doesn't mean all other motives are unimportant and that we don't care about them at all. When considering this new position in her company, she wisely reflected on other motives. I love that our Motives Circumplex makes it easy to guide you to easily touch base with other needs (again, the power of a little bit of organization structure! SO NEEDED!). Would Heather go from working forty hours a week to seventy, depleting any WORK-LIFE HARMONY? Would she go from great comfort and SECURITY to feeling insecure at work? Would she go from great PEER CONNECTION on a team of friends to a team she knew was gossipy and didn't like one another? All good things to ask yourself in her situation. Neither position was going to meet all the 28 needs equally; there would be trade-offs. Her most important motives would have been neglected and her well-being most negatively impacted if she hadn't focused her attention on meeting her top motives first and taken the job.

INTENTIONAL ACTION

"Attention has its most powerful expression in purposeful action."

—Ilchi Lee

Tending to the things that matter most in our lives doesn't just happen; intentional action is required.

> Passive can often be the default setting for our work wellness and happiness. But inaction is action; what we are not changing we are choosing.

We don't intend to be passive, but it just happens. Remember, when I was asking people questions about their or their employees' health and happiness, they would tell me a lot about their problems, but not always much about their strategy, actions, or alternative choices they were making. Many people are content at work, but if you are unhappy and your mental health is deteriorating, being in passive mode is a bigger problem. Even if your work life is good, what happens if it stops being good, which for most people inevitably happens at some point in their career? What happens when red flags start to emerge but we aren't paying attention? Why do we have to hit rock bottom burnout, be bored to death, have zero faith in our leaders, or be treated unjustly before we step up and do something? Rather than wait until things are terrible to react, maintenance and prevention are a much better way to go. You may also still be missing out on great possibilities to upgrade your quality of work life.

Heather, for example, wasn't miserable at work; she was content but already itching for more, and that itch would eventually become a burn. That's why prevention is important; rather than wait for her needs to nosedive, she was able to notice sooner than later she needed to take action based on her motive priorities. As the philosopher Desiderius Erasmus said, "Prevention is better than cure."

Being purposeful in caring for your health and happiness is also about noticing where things are going well and protecting those things as well as feeling grateful and celebrating them. In positive psychology research, gratitude is consistently linked with greater happiness, well-being, improved mental health, and less stress. Unfortunately, our human brains are wired with a negativity bias. We tend to focus on what's crappy or less than perfect rather than on what's going well. We give more weight to things that go wrong than to things that go right. It's important we have the ability for both, to not have our blinders on and pretend things are okay when they aren't, but also to focus on the positive to generate gratitude and a desired emotional experience.

I will talk more about taking intentional action to meet your motives as we walk the steps of the pathway. Mindfulness is the spark that ignites the intention.

BECOMING PURPOSEFUL WITH MY WELL-BEING

"The things which are most important don't always scream the loudest."

—Bob Hawke

I love Hawke's quote because it illuminates one of the reasons why our assessment is so important. I helped analyze the research and build the algorithm, yet I only had a confident guess of what two of my top 5 motives would be. And one was a surprise, a blind spot that sure didn't scream the loudest, yet it was the one out of my top 5 motives that was not well met. That motive was the weakest and needed my attention the most of any.

I first took the Motives Met Assessment back in 2020, right after we had finished our R&D research and perfected the algorithm.

Image 6.2 shows the motives that were most motivating and essential to me at that time.

THE MOTIVES CIRCUMPLEX™

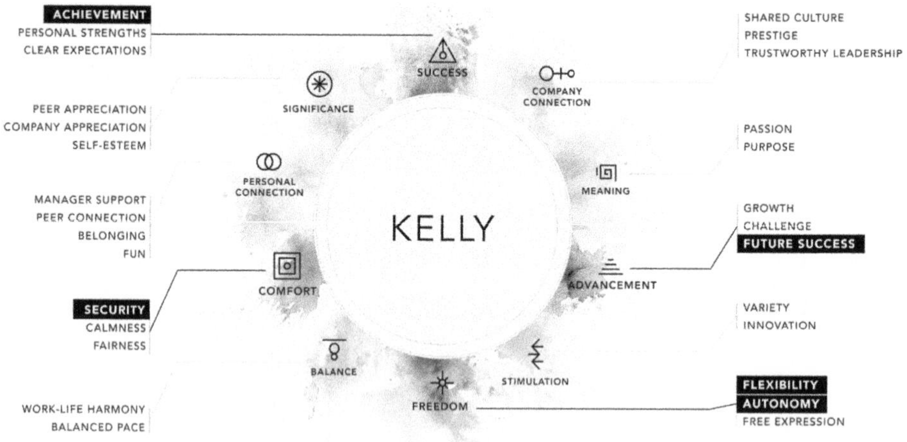

ACHIEVEMENT
PERSONAL STRENGTHS
CLEAR EXPECTATIONS

SHARED CULTURE
PRESTIGE
TRUSTWORTHY LEADERSHIP

SUCCESS

SIGNIFICANCE

COMPANY
CONNECTION

PEER APPRECIATION
COMPANY APPRECIATION
SELF-ESTEEM

PASSION
PURPOSE

PERSONAL
CONNECTION

MEANING

MANAGER SUPPORT
PEER CONNECTION
BELONGING
FUN

KELLY

GROWTH
CHALLENGE
FUTURE SUCCESS

COMFORT

ADVANCEMENT

SECURITY
CALMNESS
FAIRNESS

VARIETY
INNOVATION

BALANCE

STIMULATION

WORK-LIFE HARMONY
BALANCED PACE

FREEDOM

FLEXIBILITY
AUTONOMY
FREE EXPRESSION

Image 6.2. Kelly's motives 2020

AUTONOMY and FLEXIBILITY are part of the Freedom Domain, and after feeling stuck for so many years, freedom is tightly bound to my values, which is why these are the two I had a gut feeling might make it into my top 5. SECURITY felt like a slap in the face; that was my blind spot motive. Needing security was out of character for an adventurous, entrepreneurial risk-taker soul like me, but that motive made total sense as I reflected. I wanted to be free from the weight of too much worry and doubt, which I was experiencing a lot of, and instead feel stability and certainty in the path I was walking to build Motives Met.

To be honest, I was scared shitless in the beginning. I was walking away from comfort and financial stability to pursue my dream. It was also the weakest-met motive that I had to have a come-to-Jesus moment with; more on that later. ACHIEVEMENT and FUTURE SUCCESS made all the sense in the world. I was determined to achieve our mission of creating a better work world and have also always been an ambitious goal-driven soul by nature.

Image 6.3 shows my motives today, and image 6.4 displays my motives in 2020 and 2024 side by side.

THE MOTIVES CIRCUMPLEX™

ACHIEVEMENT
PERSONAL STRENGTHS
CLEAR EXPECTATIONS

PEER APPRECIATION
COMPANY APPRECIATION
SELF-ESTEEM

MANAGER SUPPORT
PEER CONNECTION
BELONGING
FUN

SECURITY
CALMNESS
FAIRNESS

WORK-LIFE HARMONY
BALANCED PACE

SUCCESS
SIGNIFICANCE
COMPANY CONNECTION
PERSONAL CONNECTION
MEANING

KELLY

COMFORT
ADVANCEMENT
BALANCE
FREEDOM
STIMULATION

SHARED CULTURE
PRESTIGE
TRUSTWORTHY LEADERSHIP

PASSION
PURPOSE

GROWTH
CHALLENGE
FUTURE SUCCESS

VARIETY
INNOVATION

FLEXIBILITY
AUTONOMY
FREE EXPRESSION

Image 6.3. Kelly's motives 2024

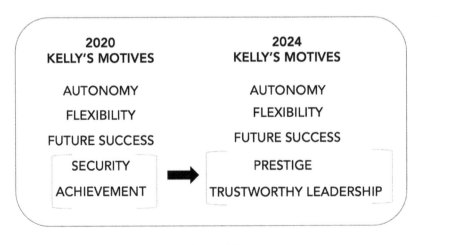

2020
KELLY'S MOTIVES

AUTONOMY

FLEXIBILITY

FUTURE SUCCESS

SECURITY

ACHIEVEMENT

2024
KELLY'S MOTIVES

AUTONOMY

FLEXIBILITY

FUTURE SUCCESS

PRESTIGE

TRUSTWORTHY LEADERSHIP

Image 6.4

I still have AUTONOMY, FLEXIBILITY, and FUTURE SUCCESS . . . but ACHIEVEMENT and SECURITY have been replaced by two motives in the Company Connection Domain, PRESTIGE and TRUSTWORTHY LEADERSHIP.

Here's how my motives have changed:

SECURITY and ACHIEVEMENT MOTIVES— No Longer in My Top 5 Motives

- When I first took the assessment, Motives Met was in its infancy. I had fears and doubts that have since subsided. I have shifted from insecurity to SECURITY, and I have also succeeded in bringing in revenue, making impact, and reaching goals, meeting my need for ACHIEVEMENT. Both of these motives have become less important for me to focus my attention and resources on.

FUTURE SUCCESS MOTIVE—Still in My Top 5 Motives

- Of greater importance now is the big dreams for the future, and if I don't feel I am on that path to FUTURE SUCCESS, my well-being will suffer, which is why this motive is still a primary driver.

PRESTIGE and TRUSTWORTHY LEADERSHIP MOTIVES—New Motives in My Top 5

- I have worked incredibly hard to create Motives Met, and it's important to me that we are a prestigious company. Feelings of pride are a big driver for PRESTIGE, and I feel so proud of what we have built. I admire our mission, and the more that people who work with us and for us do too, I find incredibly motivating and vital for my well-being.

- I have always taken on leadership roles throughout my work and personal life, but I find myself now in a bigger leadership role than I ever have before. With my immense need to be the best leader I can be, TRUSTWORTHY LEADERSHIP is a top motive. Over the last few years I have witnessed both the amazing and detrimental impact leaders are having on the health and happiness of their employees, so it's a value that has grown stronger in me.

It was important for me to contemplate why my needs had changed and to shift focus to be mindful of my vital need for PRESTIGE and TRUSTWORTHY LEADERSHIP in my work life.

Becoming mindful with your motives puts you in the driver's seat of creating the work life you want.

PUTTING INSIGHTS INTO ACTION

HARNESS THE THREE A's

Now that you have taken the assessment and can be mindful of your motives, take some time to think about how harnessing the three A's will empower you moving forward. Following are some journaling prompts to guide you:

- Is there a motive in your top 5 that was a blind spot?
- Which of your motives do you feel you had least conscious awareness around?
- In what ways have you been taking a more passive or reactive approach with meeting some of your motives?
- How do you want to change that moving forward?

CHAPTER 7

WELL-BEING IS CO-CREATED

Here's the truth: If we want well-being at work, we need to show up on purpose *with* purpose, not only for ourselves but for one another. Thinking about your top 5 motives, I'm sure you can reflect on times in your work life when others have helped support those motives and when they have hurt them. I'm sure you can also think of times when you have been that person for others. Dream Killer #6—that we tend to take a passive or reactive approach to health and happiness at work—extends beyond us and into our relationships, whether that's our work peers or the people we manage or lead; we can be more mindless than mindful.

If we want our best work lives, work relationships, and workplaces, we need to be mindful of one another's motives. The same three A's apply—being consciously *aware*, paying *attention*, and taking intentional *action*. It's asking yourself, does the way I show up at work elevate rather than harm the 28 motives? Do I have unconscious biases I should be aware of (FAIRNESS)? Do I inspire people to find joy in what they do (PASSION)? Do I vent my stress on others in unhealthy ways (CALMNESS)?

You can become more purposeful in how you generally support motives, but knowing the top motives of the people you work closest with is an even better gateway to stronger relationships, understanding, and connection. This goes for you and your boss as well; they are human too with human needs, and while they need to understand you, you also will benefit from understanding them. It's about paying attention to the things that matter, not about remembering everyone's motives. But once you know and understand others' needs and important information related to them, you can take that learning and apply it to how to work better together, support them, communicate more effectively, approach situations with them, or have greater compassion.

MINDFUL INTERACTIONS ARE A MUST

I was sometimes surprised in Motives Met workshops by how little people knew about one another and leaders knew about their employees, as it related to motives, and also how seldom these issues had been discussed at all. People may know someone's personality type or work style from another assessment they have done—whether they are an introvert or extrovert, the vacations they went on, or what they did over the weekend—but not about the things that matter most to them. That's why the Motives Met Human Needs Assessment™ is so helpful to create a self-*awareness* and also an "other-*awareness*." With this knowledge, you have greater consciousness of your human needs and the emotions intertwined with them and of the needs and emotions of other people at work. This collective awareness is powerful because well-being is co-created; we need one another to help meet our motives.

WELL-BEING IS CO-CREATED

Image 7.1

The degree a motive can be met will be influenced by other people. Put any motive in the middle of the Co-Creation Model in image 7.1 and you can imagine how multiple people will impact the degree it's met.

- If you have the BALANCED PACE motive, you might need to better manage your own time. But also communicate the optimal pace you work at and set boundaries so you have the appropriate time you need to deliver your best work on important deliverables, rather than being rushed. You will also need others to then respect those boundaries and not set time-lines without having a conversation with you first to make sure they're realistic. Be open to problem-solving to see how you can compromise on timing if necessary.

- If you have the GROWTH motive, you shouldn't expect new desired opportunities to land at your feet. You need to seek them out, ask if you can be considered for a new project, take the lead on something, or work on a different part of the business. Others need to be open to seeing you in new ways, be willing to give you a chance to grow in new areas, and provide growth-oriented feedback to help you.

- If you have the SELF-ESTEEM motive, you may want to reflect on the unique value you feel you can bring to the table, and identify your untapped potential that would make a meaningful difference to your team. Others will need to value your desire to contribute, appreciate you, and be open to your thoughts and ideas.

- If you have the INNOVATION motive and want to experiment with new ways of doing things, you may need to work through your limiting beliefs on failure. You also may need others around you to remind you that you don't fail; you succeed or you learn. Others may need to be willing to put in some extra work to experiment with trying a new way. Is your team willing to take a risk for the sake of INNOVATION? Is your work peer going to look down on you if your idea doesn't work?

I want to make the point that we use the term "work peers" intentionally here in our model. Not coworkers or teammates, because the clients, customers, and partners you work with can have just as much of an effect on motives (or more!) than the people on your team in your organization.

The idea that we can't go it alone can be comforting. The effort is joint and the responsibility shared. But that same notion can honestly also suck. It means surrendering to the truth that you only have so much control. You must take profound responsibility and ownership for your quality of work life while also accepting the effect that others will have on it. Fully accepting this truth can feel crappy because the impact from others isn't always positive. We often aren't mindful of others' motives, and we may not show compassion and support.

Dream Killer #7:
*We don't show up in meaningful ways to
co-create well-being together.*

You may speak up and set boundaries, but others don't honor them. You may try to relate to someone on your team to get along, but they hold grudges and have no interest in keeping the peace. You may go above and beyond at work, but your boss doesn't seem to notice or reward your efforts.

Companies struggle in the same way. Organizations and leaders must take that same profound responsibility for the well-being of their people, yet they also cannot control everything and everyone. You may be a leader trying to change norms in your culture, but other leaders won't get on board, which limits your impact. You could be a manager who sees that connection is lacking on your team, but a few employees have a personality, lack of work ethic, or poor character that make team members not want to work with them.

Whether we like it or not, we need each other. While not having complete control over your motives can feel hard at times, the co-creation of well-being can also be a great benefit. Others can be a huge asset to lifting up your motives, and you to others if you want to be. Part of what blocks the ability to do this is we don't all share the same mindset around health and happiness at work.

There may be common themes, but as I shared previously, people's thoughts and attitudes vary, and the truth of how to achieve well-being isn't universal. People interpret well-being in different ways, and a lack of shared meaning limits the collective well-being that can be attained. Having shared meaning with the people in your life on anything important leads to better communication and stronger relationships—and work is no exception. When we focus on motives, we benefit from shared meaning and language that's missing, we honor our differences, and we gain common ground so we can support one another at work. That language part is important. We will get more into motive discussion on the *COMMUNICATE* step of the pathway, but shared vocabulary reinforces shared meaning. Melissa Doman, MA, is an organizational psychologist who shares, in her book *Yes, You Can Talk About Mental Health at Work: Here's Why (and How To Do It Really Well)*, "The language that we use helps to shape the reality we all share. It helps to shape our attitudes in how we view the world, the meanings of what we say to others, and to ourselves . . . More specifically, the words we assign to what we are thinking or feeling are important. Naming something brings it to life."[1]

Once people start thinking and talking about it the same way, once they take responsibility for the role they play for themselves and others, then they can start being mindful in their work relationships.

WE MUST EMBRACE MOTIVE DIVERSITY

If we ignore, dismiss, unfairly favor, or are biased toward some motives and not others, if we reject some of our needs or others' needs, our dream will fall short. I briefly touched on motive diversity earlier in the book, but we need to respect that all of these motives are worthy and deserve to be met. Though our attitudes may be subconscious at times, we can hold certain biases or have tunnel vision regarding motives.

OVERLOOKED:

We may overlook motives because they aren't as relevant or obvious to us.

If you are a white male who has never been treated unfairly, never been harassed or been passed up for a promotion because of your race, gender, sexual orientation, or weight, then the need for FAIRNESS may not be top of mind or something you have concerned yourself with much.

If you have a busy social life outside of your job, you may not notice the need of some work peers to be more social at work with the desire for PEER CONNECTION.

MISUNDERSTOOD:

Motives can be misunderstood because people misinterpret them.

The need to have a sense of CALMNESS at work, a healthy relationship with stress, can be one that gets misinterpreted.

I'll share an example here to bring this to life. Joanna, who is a schoolteacher for young autistic children, certainly didn't expect her job to be stress-free. She shared stories of children throwing tantrums, calling her names, and peeing on the playground. This, she said, is to be expected, "though I would be lying to say I am immune to the toll they can take on a particularly difficult week. I don't shy away from the stress of my job, but I value the way us teachers at my school handle the stress, I value that we all care about one another's mental health. That's why the CALMNESS Motive is so critical for me."

David, who works as an event coordinator for large-scale events also had CALMNESS as a top need at work. Whether coordinating parties, weddings, or other occasions, he works in a fast-paced environment. He said, "I wasn't expecting to see CALMNESS as a top motive for me. I consider myself someone who doesn't really need work to be calm. I am great under pressure, always on the go. I get motivated when the adrenaline starts kicking in, but I can see why this is something I need."

David went on to explain that he realized there was too much unnecessary stress in his job. Yes, there was always stress the day before and day of the event; unknown unexpected things were bound to happen. Yes, feeling a bit overwhelmed at the things left to do a week before an event was normal. What was not okay was the drama on his team and the lack of communication that made mistakes happen. What was not okay was an atmosphere of constant rush, people running around with their heads cut off instead of everyone knowing what they should be doing because of the lack of organization.

For David, a fast-paced environment was something he still gravitates to with the CALMNESS motive. Someone else might work best in an environment that is laid back and relaxed. Regardless, CALMNESS doesn't mean you expect no stress or for everything to be Zen at work all the time; the schoolteacher Joanna certainly didn't. Having WORK-LIFE HARMONY doesn't mean you expect to never work past five p.m. or on an occasional weekend. And the MANAGER SUPPORT motive doesn't mean you expect your supervisor to be available to support you all the time. We have to be careful not to misconstrue motives.

DISMISSED:

Motives can be dismissed because they don't seem as important.

FUN is a motive that can often be an afterthought or perceived to be low in importance. Yet some people shared with me that their need for FUN was crucial for their job satisfaction.

PEER or COMPANY APPRECIATION can be viewed as less than. People are hired to do their jobs, so why should we have to show appreciation? Yet that feeling of significance in such a big part of our lives and one of the strongest motivators and component of fulfillment for some.

An example that comes to mind is someone I worked with earlier in my career. I'm certain he would have had the need for VARIETY as part of his core motives. He was an account manager and said he preferred to work across multiple clients than with the same account. He was extremely bummed when he was moved to an account manager position on a high-profile client others coveted, but because it was a big account, it was his only one. Many thought it was odd he was upset by this; they judged his emotions because others would have loved the opportunity and the simplicity. But he was the type of person who would get bored easily, and having VARIETY with the clients he worked with and problems he solved was incredibly important for him.

WHEN WE DON'T RESPECT MOTIVE DIVERSITY, IT LEADS TO JUDGMENT

I will wholeheartedly own that I have not always supported motive diversity at work. It wasn't on purpose; we don't always realize we are doing it. But as I look back to many years ago in my career, I had judgment for and a disrespect toward some other people's needs. I expected that others should place the same importance on ACHIEVEMENT as I did in the same way. I had the mindset that needs like FAIRNESS, WORK-LIFE HARMONY, BALANCED PACE, and CALMNESS were just something that you should learn to sacrifice; you should toughen up or get out. I wasn't as understanding and compassionate as I should have been.

When someone's motive threatens our own, when it makes our day a bit less convenient, when it means extra effort or actions we would rather not take, we can start to judge. We can lean toward exclusion and negativity. We can try to change or control others. Nonjudgment and inclusion are a foundational part of mindfulness. When we stop judging, letting go of the desire to change others' motives, we free up energy to focus on things that matter and create connection. The practice of respect and letting go of the need to control naturally creates more harmonious relationships. Work devoid of drama and unhealthy friction leaves more room for collaboration, trust, and positivity. **Rather than focusing on "How do we connect?," the more important question is "How can we limit judgment?"**

WE ALL NEED TO GIVE A SHIT; WE DON'T NEED TO LOVE ONE ANOTHER

Our human instincts can steer us to look out for ourselves, and it's a message our society has brought more to the forefront today. You need to put your health and happiness first, be a little selfish, do the self-care, put your oxygen mask on first. But we should also be self-less, we should care about others, about humankind, about the dream for a better future of work for all. And it is, in fact, also a human tendency to do that.

Humans are hardwired for kindness and generosity; research shows people want to help one another and that acts of kindness not only benefit the receiver but also the giver. This truth is a paradox because more than one thing is true: We need and tend to look out for ourselves, but we also need and tend to look out for others. The modern work world, however, makes it tougher for our humanity to shine through and is, in fact, one of our dream killers. As I touched on previously, the values and virtues that tend to be stronger in our personal lives don't show up as strongly at work because of the work world we live in. When work can be busy, stressful, more isolated remotely, competitive, and even cutthroat, caring for mental, emotional, and social health takes a back seat.

I had someone ask me, "Why should we care about helping other people meet their motives?" Essentially, why give a shit?

While it kind of seems like a jerky question, it's actually a good one, because even if as humans we care for others on some level (some people more than others), even if we want to help, making the effort to show we care to support other people's well-being isn't something that always comes naturally in our current work reality. Jeffrey Pfeffer, a Stanford University professor of organizational behavior and researcher on the effects of work environments on human health and well-being, says that one of the best ways to build well-being in the workplace is to encourage people to care for each other.[2]

To be honest, I didn't always care a great deal about other people's needs at work. It's not that I didn't care in the sense that I wasn't kind or helped people when they needed it. I was quite a go-to person if you were in need, and as a manager I genuinely cared about the people who worked for me. But mostly I was busy and focused on surviving the hectic day, getting things done, and meeting deliverables. So while I focused more on me, that focus didn't include my own well-being, let alone others.

Caring is also important for people you don't like—even more so. I want to make one thing crystal clear: Helping someone better meet their motives, caring about the mental, emotional, and social health of another human, doesn't require you to be friends, agree with them, or not have any issues with that person. We can all think of a person we worked/work with that gets under our skin, who we have been harmed by, are completely opposite from, or maybe even loathe. While people can work extremely well together and have different motives, at times they can conflict in a way that makes it tough.

Three reasons stand out as to why caring about the motives of others is so beneficial for everyone.

#1—CREATES A MORE POSITIVE EMOTIONAL EXPERIENCE FOR ALL

When we can help elevate the motives of others, this brings out the best in them and creates a ripple effect. People who have healthy motives are more likely to experience positive emotions and show up at work as a better version of themselves, which is better for you. Research shows that emotions are contagious. It's easy for us to "catch" both positive and negative emotions from others. Emotional contagion means the people you are surrounded by at work have a real impact on your own emotional well-being.

#2—GROWS CONNECTION AND COMPASSION

The principle of well-wishing upon others coincides with a form of meditation called *metta* or loving-kindness meditation. In this form of meditation, you send well-wishes to yourself, to others you feel natural kindness toward, those you have difficulty with, and ultimately to all of humankind. When you have the ability to send loving-kindness to those you struggle with, you increase your capacity for connection and compassion, decrease negative emotions, and quiet your inner critic and tendency to judge. Even if someone drives you crazy, well-wishing is operating under the belief that:

- Just like me, this person is an imperfect human.

- Just like me, this person deserves health and happiness at work the way I do.

- Just like me, this person deserves for their motives to be healthy.

Sharon Salzberg, who is a world-renowned meditation teacher, author, and foremost leader of loving-kindness meditation, says, "Loving-kindness is the deep recognition that we live in an interconnected reality . . . our lives have something to do with one another. We may not like someone, or want to bring them home, but we can understand that everybody counts, everybody matters."[3] This is the attitude that creates caring work cultures. You may not "love" every person you work with, but you can show loving-kindness, you can give a shit.

And, hey, it doesn't even necessarily mean going out of your way all the time to support them, or not having conflict. But sometimes it's simply not standing in the way of a need being met. A phrase we say on our team is that at the most basic level, don't be an asshole. Sounds obvious, right? Unfortunately, the stories I hear about people being assholes at work are disturbing.

For example, when it comes to PEER CONNECTION, you don't need to go out of your way to connect if you really don't like someone, but you also don't need to bully people and gossip about them all the time. You don't need to be the reason that someone feels they don't have a true sense of BELONGING. You don't need to be the one to stifle someone's PASSION or stunt their GROWTH.

#3—LEADS TO GREATER SUPPORT FROM OTHERS

Well-being is a two-way street. More often than not, your caring will inspire caring in others.

MARIA, ER NIGHT-SHIFT NURSE

Motives: PEER CONNECTION, BELONGING, MANAGER SUPPORT, CALMNESS, SHARED CULTURE

> I started working at a new hospital and I was taken aback by the dynamic between the nurses and the overall culture. It was very much an "every man for himself" type mindset.

At my old job/hospital, when someone was rushed into the ER, anyone who was there helped. One person checked them in while another tended to their needs; it was sort of an all hands on deck. At this hospital it was the person who was "up" who mostly did it all when someone came in, while other nurses were sitting down chatting or online shopping on their cell phones.

I decided to be the change I wanted to see. Even when it wasn't "my turn," I would go to the lead nurse and see how I could help. I shared with a few of the nurses that I really appreciated in my old job that all of us nurses pitched in to make everyone's lives easier. I framed it like, hey I know I'm the new person, but this is what I've seen work well and I want to be a good coworker, so share with me how I can support you too. One person was coping with a parent who had cancer and needed shifts covered last minute at times. I volunteered to take a few of them when she asked, and you know what? She started acting less cold to me and more friendly. She started reciprocating my kindness. And while I wouldn't say the spirit is quite the same as my other colleagues, there has been a significant shift in the support and connection among us, and more often than not, others are offering to help, even when they don't have to.

When Maria started the new job, her motives were not being met, so she took action to improve her own well-being and inspire those she worked with to support these motives.

Having care, compassion, and support for other people's needs can be about simple things: It can mean putting down the online shopping for a few minutes to help, saying thank you, taking a shift for someone when they need it, or being patient when someone is trying something new. When people have motives in mind with how they think, feel, and act with one another, it has a spillover effect, and everyone wins.

PUTTING INSIGHTS INTO ACTION
DISCOVER OTHER PEOPLE'S MOTIVES

Ideally, the people you interact with in your work life would also take the assessment and know their top motives. You can also share that you took the Motives Met Human Needs Assessment™, what you learned about yourself, some of your takeaways, and see if they would want to take it. Or just ask them what they think some of their motives might be and why. It signals you are curious about them, and you value and care about them as a person. Having a discussion with your boss or other leaders around motives can be another opportunity to gain insight. It can also be a subtle nudge for those work peers or bosses who aren't so great about the whole work well-being thing—they aren't great at treating people with kindness, respecting motive diversity, or being self-aware of how they hurt motives.

EXAMINE MOTIVE STRENGTHS AND
WEAKNESSES IN YOUR RELATIONSHIPS

Take a moment to think about your work relationships, and use the following questions to guide you as you write down your thoughts:

- Can you think of a time when someone you worked with or worked for judged, minimized, or didn't respect your needs? How did that feel for you?

- Can you think of times when you were the person who didn't respect someone else's needs? If so, you might want to consider making amends and addressing your mistake with them. Do you find yourself judging, ignoring, or belittling any of the 28 motives? How are you going to change this moving forward?

- Think about the reverse. Can you think about the people in your life who have supported your needs in ways that made a positive impact? If you think they would appreciate hearing the impact they made, consider expressing your gratitude.

EVALUATE

UNDERSTAND BE MINDFUL EVALUATE COMMUNICATE MEET MOTIVES

CHAPTER 8

ARE YOUR MOTIVES MET?

The third step down the Motives Met Pathway is to *EVALUATE* motives, to really know how healthy your needs are and thus how healthy your work life is. If you want to be empowered in elevating important areas of your life, you need a clear picture of where you are now so you can get to where you want to be. When it comes to your quality of work life, that isn't an easy task. Effort is required, and even with that effort, as we know, things like health and happiness are intangible, historically something people haven't known how to define well (until now!).

Dream Killer #8
Well-being doesn't get evaluated and
measured in the way it should.

If you want to be proactive and preventive with your well-being, to show up *on* purpose *with* purpose to create your optimal work life, as we just talked about on the *BE MINDFUL* step, then you need to know the health of your motives. Thriving at work aside, we tend to not be the best "evaluators" in many areas of our lives. The busyness, the grind of day-to-day life, and the default of our automatic mode rather than mindful mode don't lend themselves naturally to stopping and truly assessing how things are going. Building systems and habits and having resources readily available help you make what I think of as "life checkups" a regular rather than rare thing.

What helps you to assess the quality of your work life is putting a number on things, to have data on yourself where you can step back and evaluate the data objectively and get curious and analytical. Measurement is part of what helps you evaluate your well-being along with self-reflection, which we will tackle in the next chapter.

HOW HEALTHY ARE YOUR MOTIVES?

Our "immeasurable" desired outcomes are often the most important, and **measuring the things that matter in life puts you in a better position to get the outcomes you want**. While health and happiness at work have traditionally been difficult to assess, they don't have to be. When you know your motives, you have clear dimensions, making the immeasurable measurable in a simple, straightforward way. You can determine the degree your motives are met, whether they are thriving, coasting, suffering, or drowning. It's evaluating the right things that matters. A popular saying is that "not everything that can be counted counts." If you are focused on assessing PASSION, or lack thereof, but it's not a core motive to your greatest work life and your more important motives are being neglected, you are missing the mark. You have to measure the right things.

"The things we measure are the things we improve. It is only through numbers and clear tracking that we have any idea if we are getting better or worse." **—James Clear**

There are many benefits to evaluating the health of your motives. You can:

- More easily hold yourself accountable.

- Have greater clarity and validation on why you feel the way you do.

- Tap into motivation when you can see noticeable momentum and progress.

- Have an effective way to communicate the state of your well-being to others.

- Catch small problems before they become big problems.

YOUR MOTIVES HEALTH SCORECARD

"Without proper self-evaluation, failure is inevitable."

—John Wooden

There are three simple steps to determining the health of your motives. This isn't a long process, and this chapter is short and sweet.

STEP 1: EVALUATE EACH OF YOUR TOP 5 MOTIVES INDIVIDUALLY TO GAUGE THE HEALTH OF THESE MOTIVES.

First, think about your motives one by one.

Considering your work life right now, how "met" are each of your top 5 motives on a 4-point scale? Are they 1) drowning, 2) suffering, 3) coasting, or 4) thriving?

MOTIVE HEALTH RATINGS

MOTIVE 1 ◯ ◯ ◯ ◯
        1 2 3 4

MOTIVE 2 ◯ ◯ ◯ ◯
        1 2 3 4

MOTIVE 3 ◯ ◯ ◯ ◯
        1 2 3 4

MOTIVE 4 ◯ ◯ ◯ ◯
        1 2 3 4

MOTIVE 5 ◯ ◯ ◯ ◯
        1 2 3 4

Image 8.1

Answer this question thinking about each motive overall in your work life, not just how you feel on this particular day. Think about a time frame that feels best to you, perhaps in the last three months of this new job or over this last year. In that time period, how met do you feel these motives are?

Below is a benchmark to help you determine your motive health.

DROWNING

Your motive is distressed. You significantly feel the negative emotional experience stemming from the lack of health for this need.

SUFFERING

Your motive is hurting, not dismal but not strong, and has ample room for improvement.

COASTING

Your motives are cruising along, coasting. You may feel simply content about these needs; they are doing okay or a bit better than okay.

THRIVING

Your motive is flourishing and strong. You significantly feel the positive emotional experience stemming from the health of this need.

MY MOTIVE HEALTH SCORECARD

I want to walk you through my evaluation of my original motives when I took the Motives Met Human Needs Assessment™ for the first time in 2020 to bring this process to life for you. One of my original motives was SECURITY. When I assessed the Motive Health criteria in my Motives Met Report, I could see it was my least healthy motive. The different sections in your report help you evaluate and reflect on the health of each motive. The motive health indicators section specifically gives you a gut check-in to work from when evaluating your motives.

Motive Health for SECURITY

(included in your Motives Met Report)

MOTIVE HEALTH INDICATORS

You feel this motive is being met when...

+You feel safe and at ease in your workplace: physically, emotionally, and psychologically.

+Your job and income are stable and dependable.

+You feel confident that you know what to expect at work.

+You have good job SECURITY, and are unlikely to lose your job due to factors outside of your control.

You feel this motive is at risk when...

– Your workplace has a high turnover rate or undergoes frequent layoffs.

– Your job currently involves a lot of unpredictability – whether around income, consistency of work, caliber of client, or shifting expectations.

– You don't feel physically, mentally, or emotionally safe at work.

– You've honestly assessed any insecurity that you feel in your job and have determined that this discomfort stems from exterior factors, not your own attitudes or internal insecurities.

Image 8.2

I had no idea what to expect on the wild ride I was beginning upon launching a startup. Safe and at ease? That was a hell no. Job security? Not so much. I was leaving behind certainty and financial stability from both my research work and my coaching practice that I would be doing less of. I was facing some not-so-great risk factors for my motive.

Thankfully, my other motives were in a better spot. This is where my motive health stood:

MOTIVE HEALTH

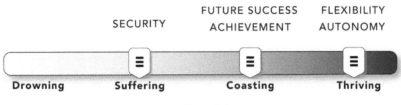

Image 8.3

DROWNING

- None

None of my motives fell into this category, but let me tell you, years ago most of them would have.

SUFFERING

- SECURITY

My SECURITY motive was weak for sure. I didn't feel it was quite drowning under water yet, but it certainly wasn't coasting.

COASTING

- ACHIEVEMENT
- FUTURE SUCCESS

ACHIEVEMENT and FUTURE SUCCESS were doing okay. Room for growth but positive momentum I felt good about.

THRIVING

- FLEXIBILITY
- AUTONOMY

FLEXIBILITY and AUTONOMY, the two motives in the Freedom Domain most tightly bound to my values, were both crushing it.

STEP 2: EVALUATE YOUR TOP 5 MOTIVES HOLISTICALLY.

When analyzing your motives, you need to think about their relationship with one another and examine them in context together. If you remember on the Motives Circumplex, motives that are closer together tend to have less friction, whereas motives farther from one another can have greater tension.

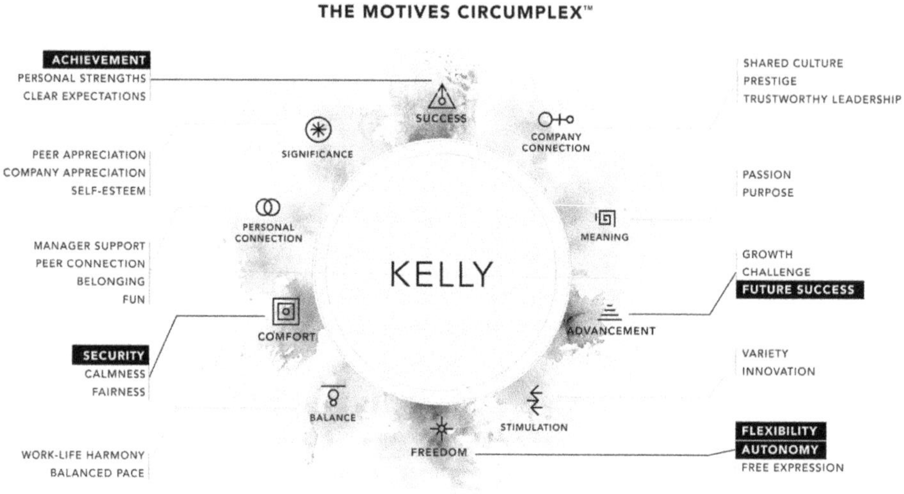

THE MOTIVES CIRCUMPLEX™

Image 8.4. Kelly Mackin's Original Motives Circumplex 2020

Given SECURITY was my weakest motive, it was particularly important to think about it in the context of my other motives. I could see that it was at odds with my need for ACHIEVEMENT and FUTURE SUCCESS. I knew that to accomplish both my short-term goals today and longer-term goals for tomorrow, I needed to befriend fear and discomfort rather than be at war with them. The problem is, the SECURITY motive lives in our comfort zone, in the Comfort Domain. How was I going to reconcile this?

When I thought about SECURITY in the context of my other

needs, I realized I didn't need this motive to be as strong as the others, even if I didn't love the way insecurity felt. If I felt super comfy, then I would be sacrificing my goals and not reaching my potential. I wouldn't be taking risks, pushing myself, and doing some of the new and exciting yet also intimidating, challenging, and scary things I wanted and needed to do.

I wanted to improve my SECURITY while also being wise to the truth that my goal wasn't to feel completely secure. When you analyze your needs holistically, you gain a different perspective. You may need to make trade-offs and hard choices. You may notice common themes or how certain motives feed into one another.

STEP 3: DECIDE HOW YOU FEEL ABOUT YOUR MOTIVES. MY WORK WELL-BEING IS . . .

Having this data on yourself allows you to decide how you feel about your work well-being overall. If I'd had this tool many years ago, I know I would have determined I had downright awful work well-being. And that would have helped me "wake up" sooner. Having the data staring you in the face makes it harder to look the other way, to avoid and pretend it's not happening. I touched on this as one of the benefits from evaluating your motives: facing uncomfortable truths. **Evaluating your motives and having a "carefrontation" with yourself can change your life.**

The purpose is not to stew in feeling bad about your well-being if it's not where you want it to be; it's to use this information to create a new beginning, to take the first steps toward a better work life.

In 2020, when I first evaluated my well-being using this process, I felt my well-being was strong and I was motivated by how far I had come. This is an important step because, as we just tackled in step 2, you may not need all motives to be thriving right now; it may not even be realistically possible for that to happen and that's okay. My SECURITY motive was suffering. I didn't need it to be thriving, but could I work to get it to be coasting? That was the goal. I also hoped that my needs for ACHIEVEMENT and FUTURE SUC-CESS would shift from coasting to a thriving place. When creating your Work Life Well-Lived Action Plan that we will tackle in the last step of the pathway, you want to think about the health of your motives now and where you want them to be, and what actions will help you bridge the gap from where you are now to where you want to be. It could simply mean changing your attitude, asking someone for help, or making a huge or even a tiny change.

Today, my Motive Health Scorecard is even higher. What's cool is I know where my work health and happiness stands, but beyond that I also know *why*. It isn't measuring on a scale just how happy I feel at work or how much fulfillment I think I have. Saying I'm at an 8 out of 10 on feeling happy doesn't help me a whole lot. It's being able to know I am thriving today because my top needs are met and knowing exactly what those are.

PUTTING INSIGHTS INTO ACTION
DETERMINE THE HEALTH OF YOUR MOTIVES

Take a few minutes and go through the evaluation process for your motives to develop your Motives Health Scorecard. Remember, you can use your Motives Met Report to guide you!

COMMUNICATE

UNDERSTAND | BE MINDFUL | EVALUATE | COMMUNICATE | MEET MOTIVES

CHAPTER 9

CREATING YOUR
MOTIVE STORY

The fourth step down the Motives Met Pathway is to *COMMUNICATE* about motives, having conversations with yourself and others regarding motives at work. These important conversations can be lacking, and there are many reasons for this silence. Maybe your busy schedule inhibits a reflective chat with yourself about your needs, or the fact you aren't the most introspective person by nature. It could be the way your stomach clenches when you think about telling your boss your motives are hurting. It could be the fact that people on your team don't really talk about this stuff. It can also be a result of the lack of common language we have historically had to talk about these things with one another.

We need to talk about motives to meet them, but one of the biggest barriers is that they are a missing conversation.

Dream Killer #9:
We don't talk about what we need most
at work with ourselves and others.

COMMUNICATION WITH SELF

"We do not learn from experience. We learn from reflecting
on experience."
—John Dewey

Reflection is where much learning happens. It's where we weed through our experiences, consider alternative perspectives, engage in deliberate thought, generate new ideas, and experience break-throughs. But it isn't always fun to do. Some people are more reflective by nature and enjoy journaling, for example. For others it's more of a chore, not top of mind, or easy to procrastinate on. There is also the avoidance we talked about in the *EVALUATE* step on the Motives Met Pathway, when we know motives are weak but we aren't immediately sure how to solve them, so we turn a blind eye.

Even once you have committed to the practice of reflection, the question becomes, What exactly should I reflect upon? While we reflect to get answers, the most powerful answers come in the form of asking yourself thought-provoking questions, to be curious about yourself. There are specific questions for each of your motives to get those reflection juices flowing in your Motives Met Report, but you might want more reflection time with some of your motives than with others. The Motive Reflection Questions section of the report is my personal favorite, as these questions deliver truth bombs, aha moments, and new ideas as to how you can strengthen your motives. I'll share a few questions from my Motives Met Report to give you an idea.

SECURITY MOTIVE

Motive Reflection Question: What aspects of my work life are most secure? Do I focus there or only on where I feel insecure? What mindset can I cultivate to help me meet this motive?

Answer: I spent a good amount of reflection time on my SECURITY motive because, as I've said, I rated it as a "suffering" motive in my Motives Health Scorecard. This was such a simple but important question for me to think about. I was letting my brain sit in a pool of insecurity without redirecting it to all the ways my work life was secure. I had a great work ethic, experience, and skill set for anything I wanted to do in the future. I knew people both needed and wanted a solution like Motives Met. While it was financially scary, I knew I could make it work for a short period of time. I would be doing less work in my research and coaching, but those were things I could always come back to if I needed to. I also reminded myself, isn't one of the benefits of going on this entrepreneurial journey to have greater long-term SECURITY? Building a company of my own allows me to secure my own livelihood. It became even more clear that much of protecting this motive was going to be protecting my mindset.

FUTURE SUCCESS MOTIVE

Motive Reflection Question: When I think about my future self who has the success I desire, in what ways are they similar or different from me today? (What is their mindset? How do they feel at work? Where do they invest their time and energy? How do they make decisions? What habits do they have?) How do I need to become more like my future self today to create the future I desire?

Answer: This question is so dang motivating to me, I come back to it often. If I want the career that my future self has, I can't just wait to have the things come to me. The future me brings focused energy to everything I do. The future me does uncomfortable things all the time. The future me prioritizes the work that will create the greatest impact, not less important work that feels urgent but really isn't. The future me cares less about things that don't matter but cares a lot about the things that do matter. I need to show up as that person today; I need to think, feel, and act the way my future self thinks, feels, and acts.

FLEXIBILITY MOTIVE

Motive Reflection Question: What would my ideal workday look like? Do I have enough FLEXIBILITY to arrange most, some, or none of my workdays to look like this?

Answer: FLEXIBILITY is a thriving, well-met motive for me, but this was still interesting to contemplate, especially back in 2020 when I first took the assessment. By then I worked remotely and had the ability to bend my schedule to my needs. I had so much FLEXI-BILITY after I used to have very little. It felt good to sit in that truth for a moment, to acknowledge how great it is that I had the freedom I had always desired. What was also true is I didn't always use it to its full advantage; I felt guilty or lazy not being at my desk in the typical workday time slot. I thought about what my ideal days did look like: How was I going to make the most out of my FLEXIBILITY to support those types of days?

Those days included time to do deep, creative work toward my bigger goals for my FUTURE SUCCESS motive. They included shutting down my computer early if it was a beautiful afternoon and doing something outside. Not all days would be like that. Some days I had workshops, internal meetings, or client meetings that took up most of the hours. But I could in fact have more days like that if I was more intentional in how I designed my schedule because I did have a lot of FLEXIBILITY to work with. As part of my Work Life Well-Lived Action Plan, which you will develop on the last step of the pathway, I decided to carve out two days a week where I had no meetings (or limited meetings if need be) where I started work at five a.m., and by midafternoon I had put in more than a full day of deep, creative work and had the rest of the day to do other things.

When you take the time to go inward, to reflect, and to have a chat with yourself, you are prioritizing your health and happiness, and your motives will benefit.

MOTIVE STORIES

We all have a story behind our motives. You have had so many experiences in your work life in your past, are living in the truth of your current job reality today, and are carrying the hopes for tomorrow.

> Crafting your motive story helps you to further reflect and make sense of all of that, organize your experiences, and create meaning.

Research shows that storytelling is linked with greater mental health and well-being benefits.[1] Stories can help to heal, can help you feel empowered, and are meant to be shared with others. One of the copywriters on our team experienced this being part of Motives Met and specifically found formulating her motive story very therapeutic. She also had a tale to tell of work wounds from her past but said the work at Motives Met made her feel validated and helped her heal from that past. She deserved to be human. She was right when she pursued a job path where her needs were met, even though at the time it felt like she may have been making the wrong decision. Developing your story propels you forward and helps you crystalize your Work Life Well-Lived Action Plan.

When you share your motive story with others, it's a powerful way to connect. As I have explained to others my strong value for freedom in my work life with my FLEXIBILITY and AUTONOMY motives and why that value is so important to me, team members have said they felt like they got to know another part of me and also opened up to share their similar situations with me. Even my mom learned new things about me, and I learned new things about her, too. She laughed as I shared some of my meaning behind my FLEXIBILITY motive and said, "I always saw you as the taskmaster since that's what one of your clients named you years ago, and the name can certainly fit! Sometimes you seemed to lean more rigid to me than flexible in things like your schedule, or ways of doing things. But I realize now that you need to be your own taskmaster and have the flexibility to work toward your goals in the best way for you." Ironically, I need the FLEXIBILITY to be rigid with myself. Ultimately, storytelling about our motives helps us find common ground while honoring differences and creating deeper bonds in our work relationships.

I've been sharing some of my own and others' motive stories throughout the book already, so by now you get the gist. But I want to make reflection as easy as possible and give you ideas to help craft your motive narrative. At the end of your Motives Met Report, we guide you through a few prompts to help you write your story, and I will also walk through them with you now. These are prompts to get you thinking, and you don't need to answer all of them. Your motive story is your own. You can focus where you wish, whether it's on motives that are in greatest distress, or on parts that excite you the most.

CRAFTING YOUR MOTIVE STORY

Since you have heard quite a bit of my motive story throughout these pages, I thought I would share my mom's story with you as I take you through the different elements. The motives driving my mother, Mary Mackin's, well-being are: ACHIEVEMENT, PEER APPRE-CIATION, SELF-ESTEEM, BELONGING, and FAIRNESS. See image 9.1.

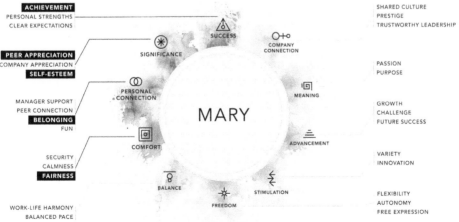

Image 9.1

1. PERSONAL MEANING

Motives are in the eye of the beholder, and it's valuable to think about what your motives mean to you.

- How would you describe each as it relates to your current work life, past, and hopes for the future?

- What does it say about you that these motives are vital for you to thrive at work?

- Where do you find connection and synergies between your motives, and where do you find disconnection and friction?

Mary Mackin's Story

"My motives are toward the left side of the Motives Circumplex. BELONGING, PEER APPRECIATION, and SELF-ESTEEM in particular have a lot in common and show that my relationships with other work peers are essential to me being most fulfilled. It may sound cliché, but I have always been a team player—even as a kid I loved being part of a team; maybe it was being in the middle of six kids and always trying to make sure everyone was getting along! To me, the need for SELF-ESTEEM is driven by wanting to add real value for our team and our mission for a better work world. When others share that they appreciate my work, it's a sign to me that I am adding value. PEER APPRECIATION helps reinforce I am a pivotal team player.

"Feeling significant to others has always added to my esteem and happiness, but it also feeds my desire for BELONGING. I can see a pattern where I have felt most fulfilled in my career when I was part of an inclusive team. I value a team dynamic where people feel they can be themselves. Even as I think about ACHIEVEMENT, that need is also driven by the team; my goals aren't about my own personal goals as much, but our collective goals. It's important to me to know that I am contributing to that in a meaningful way."

2. IDENTIFY THE "WHY"

What is the "why" behind your motives? Why is a motive pivotal for your work well-being? For example, is a motive of top importance because it's . . .

- Tied to a specific outcome or goal? Aspirational and forward looking?

- Linked with positive or negative experiences from your past?

- Value-based, one that is woven into your personal values and sense of self?

- Threatened or severely suffering and desperately needs tending to so it's grown in importance?

- Specifically connected to where you are in your personal life right now? Or a new significant change in any part of your life?

- A "deal-breaker" motive, something you feel you cannot or will not work without?

Mary Mackin's Story

"FAIRNESS is a driving motive for many reasons, but primarily it's a value-based motive for me. I've always been an advocate for doing the right thing and treating others fairly. I too often assumed that others valued this as much as I did and believed I would be treated fairly when I wasn't. I learned not to assume others value this motive and to ask questions and increase my awareness to see if they really do. My past work experience made me even more invested in the importance of working with others who value this motive the same way I do, so this one also feels like a 'deal-breaker' motive. I would never work with others again who are not extremely fair-minded."

3. STRENGTHS, STRUGGLES, AND SHARING

It's important to think about strengths and weaknesses surrounding your motives and what parts of your story are most beneficial to share with others.

Strengths:

Reflect on the positives. What's going well, and what desired outcomes do you have in your work life connected to your motives?

- Something I like about myself or about the way I work because of my motive(s) is . . .

- The motive I feel most grateful for is . . .

- A motive that I'm grateful that my company, manager, team, or work peers are good at supporting is . . .

- The motive I do the best at honoring is . . .

- I discovered something new about myself because of my motive(s), which is . . .

Struggles:

Identify the weaknesses, what is not going well, and the unwanted results related to your motives.

- One current challenge to a motive being fully met is . . .
- The motive I struggle the most with is . . .
- One of my motives that I often feel is judged, misunderstood, or dismissed is . . .
- My motives that are at odds or hold tension with one another are . . .
- The motive that needs the most support from others is . . .
- A motive I may need to compromise right now for the sake of my other motives is . . .

Sharing:

Determine what you could share with others that would lead to deeper understanding and benefit your motives.

- A valuable thing for me to share with others about my motives/ my story is . . .
- Something new my work peers or my boss probably don't know about me as it relates to my motives is . . .
- An example of a time my motives were met or not met that would be helpful to share with others is . . .

Mary Mackin's Story

"I feel a lot of gratitude for the health of all my motives—they are all strong, something I would not have been able to say years ago! In particular, BELONGING is the motive I feel the strongest connection and gratitude for because I get the most special experience of getting to be on a team with my daughter. In the past few years, we have also been able to partner with one of my old bosses who I have known for many years. Being part of such a close-knit team and getting to work with so many good people at Motives Met has been amazing.

"ACHIEVEMENT is where I struggle the most. It's a 'cruising' motive, not in the suffering or drowning bucket, but the motive that needs the most improvement. I have played a significant role in bringing Motives Met to life, but as we started to grow, some of the goals we needed to reach started to drift outside of my personal expertise. I had moments of feeling like I wasn't helping to achieve as much as I would like for my team, which then started to seep into my SELF-ESTEEM, too. Sharing this with the team was helpful. We all had to determine where we could best put our time and energy to reach our milestones and where we needed to start getting outside support and bring new people in. I had to reground myself in areas where I could add the most value and accept that in certain areas, I wouldn't be able to help as much. As our team reminded me, this is a good sign: Growth meant we were collectively achieving more."

PUTTING INSIGHTS INTO ACTION

HAVE A MOTIVE CHAT WITH YOURSELF

Carve out some uninterrupted time to have a conversation with yourself about your motives, using your Motives Met Report; think through the Motive Reflection Questions, and develop your motive story. You don't need to answer all of the reflection questions for each motive, but find the questions that resonate most with you. These questions get you going, but they will most likely lead to other questions or thoughts you want to reflect on as well. It's especially important to spend some time on less-met motives that you rated as drowning or suffering in your Motive Health Scorecard in the last chapter. You can access the online worksheet at motivesmet.com/book-resources.

CHAPTER 10

TALKING ABOUT WHAT MATTERS MOST

W e don't usually walk up to one another at work and say things like, "Let's chat about what you need so you can be your best at work. How can I support you and how can you support me in my well-being?" Sometimes we don't talk about motives because we feel vulnerable or uncomfortable. Other times we are busy or default to typical small talk and miss talking about the deeper stuff. Per Dream Killer #9, motives are a missing convo at work.

To create work cultures where motives are strong and mindful relationships happen, we must know one another's motives as the first step; but knowing them isn't enough. We need to talk about them.

> When we discuss motives, when they are out in the open, only then can they be protected, healed, enhanced, and praised.

That's how we get to know one another as human beings, grow our compassion, do things that support motives, and stop doing the things that don't. That is how we build that human culture of care where everyone gives a shit.

TALKING ABOUT THE STUFF THAT MATTERS

One of the first workshops we did early on at Motives Met was with a team at a smaller product company that was growing quickly, and it's always been a really great example of how powerful simply knowing and talking about motives with work peers can be. Two people—Dave and Jae—discovered their different motives had been driving a disconnect between them.

Dave has the SECURITY motive. He is more cautious by nature, has the tendency to play it safe, and is an analytical thinker. He is responsible for a lot of the budgeting and forecasting decisions. Jae has the INNOVATION motive. She is a big thinker and creator, was one of the first on the team at the startup, and was responsible for many successful ideas. Whenever Jae brought a new idea to the table she was excited about, she felt Dave was always the first to shut her ideas down. Rather than respond with optimism or enthusiasm when she got excited about a new possibility, Dave would automatically start asking questions and lead with worst-case-scenario thinking.

Dave and Jae began to understand how the needs that drove their perspectives and behaviors were clashing. Dave could see that while his need for SECURITY was valid, his approach could be demotivating for Jae. He needed to allow people to get excited about an idea, show appreciation for the new solutions being offered, and if it was something they wanted to pursue further, there was a time and place to think through both best- and worst-case scenarios. Jae agreed to honor the importance for more concrete budgets so they were being financially smart.

A lot of great stuff manifests from getting teams, managers, and organizations together to talk about motives. But many don't. If you hold a certain position as a team lead or manager, you have the ability to get people together to have these discussions. If you aren't in that position, you can suggest that this is something that would be good for your team to do. You can also be the one to simply start motive conversations. You can ask people what they find FUN about the work you do or how they most feel appreciated at work in support of PEER APPRECIATION. You can start up a conversation around the big goals peers are working toward for their FUTURE SUC-CESS or the best ways to communicate with them to honor their WORK-LIFE HARMONY.

Talking about motives can lead to the following good outcomes.

CREATES AUTHENTIC CONNECTION

Our human brains are wired for stories. Stories bind us together, and when we share them, we feel seen and validated. When we hear them, it evokes emotion and expands our compassion. Stories are also an influential way to get others to understand our perspective. Facts and figures are important, but they don't move us emotionally and persuade us the way a story can.

Learning more about who someone is as a person can ignite connection. In talking about motives with someone, we inevitably connect with them as a human person, not just a "work person." Hearing about our coworkers' lives and needs outside of work and how that integrates with their motives at work can change the way we support and relate to them.

PSYCHOLOGICAL SAFETY, TRUST, AND VULNERABILITY CAN GROW

Psychological safety—where people confidently feel they can communicate, be vulnerable, bring up uncomfortable truths, and generally be themselves without fear or worry—is critical to well-being at work, along with trust and vulnerability. You aren't going to talk candidly and honestly about your needs if you feel it will come back to hurt you.

An important aspect of effective reflection about your motives is being inquisitive and asking yourself questions, and it's just as important to bring a curious attitude when you interact with others. In a research study, Professor Alison Brooks, who had been studying conversations at Harvard Business School, came to the conclusion that people do not ask enough questions. "In fact, among the most common complaints people make after having a conversation, such as an interview, a first date, or a work meeting, is 'I wish [s/he] had asked me more questions' and 'I can't believe [s/he] didn't ask me any questions.'"[1]

Asking people questions about their motives shows interest. It puts you in learning mode rather than judgment mode. If you are truly open and curious, it's an invitation for people to answer with greater vulnerability even if the question isn't incredibly comfortable. I sometimes think of questions as invitations to answers we wouldn't give otherwise. Curiosity can lead to places we didn't expect. Another positive? Research shows that asking others questions leaves a positive impression and makes you more likable.[2]

When people have candid dialogue around their needs and share their motive stories, they are also becoming more familiar with one another, getting to know one another under the surface, and that is a gigantic builder of trust. As human behavior researchers, our team has been studying trust in relationships for years, and one of the biggest factors of trust we discovered from our research is depth of familiarity. Not just awareness, but I have the perception that I know you well. The greater depth of familiarity, the greater trust that can be built. Of course, there are other factors. I have to feel good about what I know; if I discover you are a liar, that makes me more certain you are untrustworthy. But the more I understand you as a person and feel you understand me, the more trust is possible between us even if we don't see completely eye to eye on things.

HELPS STRENGTHEN RELATIONSHIPS AND OUTCOMES

You aren't going to remember everyone's top motives, nor do you need to. I've had so many people share their top motives with me, I definitely don't remember everyone's top 5. But if you talk about them, you will be able to remember things that are important, and they will also extract important things about you. You may remember one or two of their motives you particularly want to be mindful of. Maybe hearing their story builds greater familiarity and thus trust between you, or it just offers you a new but important perspective of a person and a commonality that helps you work better together.

Motive stories help us learn and also remember. Jennifer Aaker, a marketing professor at the Stanford Graduate School of Business, says that people remember information when it is woven into stories "up to 22 times more than facts alone."[3]

HELPS US TO GET AND GIVE SUPPORT

People aren't mind readers, which is why communication in relationships is so important. Others are not going to automatically know what you need, nor will you know what others need all the time. Sometimes this falls into uncommunicated expectations—you assume that someone knows how important something is to you or you expect they will handle something the way you would. To get the right support and to give the right support, we must be willing to clearly communicate expectations, where and how we could use support, AND we must also listen. It's not just talk and take, but listen and give. Being clear communicators and explicit in how our motives can be supported comes with its challenges, which we will talk more about shortly.

WE GET TO HEAR ABOUT THE GOOD STUFF

Yes, there can be problems surrounding motives, but there is also a lot of good stuff happening too. Did it feel good when someone had your back and stood up for you when you were overlooked for an opportunity because you are the youngest on the team (FAIRNESS)? Is someone you work with really good at staying calm under pressure, and that helps you to also stay calm under pressure (CALMNESS)? Did your company recognize the hard work you and your team contributed in a way that was meaningful (COMPANY APPRECIATION)? Does one of your coworkers plan a lot of activities and gatherings that offer social opportunities you value (PEER CONNECTION)?

It benefits everyone to focus on the positive, to know what's going well and what to do more of, and hearing positive feedback makes them to want to do more of it in the future.

WE HAVE OPPORTUNITIES TO PROBLEM-SOLVE

We have to talk about the good and the bad. Obviously, you can't solve invisible problems. When needs are regularly discussed, issues are more likely to surface and unmet motives will come to light—which is a good thing. When they remain below the surface, they wreak more havoc and become bigger problems that will eventually implode. At times, people will have motives that conflict, and they'll need to compromise. Negotiating with motives in mind can help you compromise in ways that actually solve problems.

The more motives are talked about, the more mindful everyone can be with motives, the more the three A's expand—conscious **awareness**, focused **attention**, and intentional **action**. A caveat is, if communication isn't good, these benefits won't happen. Bravery is required to have conversations that can at times be uncomfortable.

COURAGEOUS COMMUNICATION

There are three main steps to being courageous with your motive communication.

1. BE SELECTIVELY VULNERABLE

"Staying vulnerable is a risk we have to take if we want to experience connection."   **—Brené Brown**

As Brené Brown, the queen of vulnerability, says, you need to take off your workplace armor if you want to truly connect. But let's face it, talking about aspects of your motives with others can be downright scary and intimidating. Sharing that you don't think a fellow leader is being an admirable one (TRUSTWORTHY LEADERSHIP), that you aren't able to do your job well because someone on the team isn't doing their part and it's inhibiting your goals (ACHIEVEMENT), or that your coworker is trying to boss you around and tell you what to do when they aren't the boss and it's not cool (AUTONOMY) can make you feel vulnerable. Unfortunately—I won't lie to you—it isn't completely safe all the time to share all you would like to share. I wish I could tell you it was, but I know some of you are on psychologically unsafe teams or work with or for untrustworthy people.

Brené Brown teaches that vulnerability is not about guaranteed outcomes, it's about showing up with courage without being in control of what happens. It's often worth the risk to be vulnerable; it's a bedrock of trust, strong relationships, and a pivotal part of meeting motives. Whether it's "worth the risk" is a personal question only you can answer, which is why to me the key is selective vulnerability, knowing the benefits of allowing yourself to be vulnerable while also being wise as to how much you share and with whom.

2. ASK FOR WHAT YOU NEED

"Ask for help. Not because you are weak. But because you want to remain strong." **—Les Brown**

When we don't vocalize our needs, we become detached from them, and they remain unmet or undermet. Ask others for what you need. Seems simple, yeah? But discomfort around asking for support from others is common and stops us from actually doing it, partially because you may have to be vulnerable.

At times asking for motive support can be easy. "I've been brainstorming some new ideas that I think would help our team be more efficient. Would you have a few minutes this week where I can run them by you to get your opinion?" (INNOVATION). Or, "I've felt cooped up working from home all week. Anyone want to meet for lunch on Friday?" (PEER CONNECTION). Other times, asking for favors, changes in behavior or help, and saying no can feel more uncomfortable, scary, or intimidating. You might need to tell your manager, "I don't have the bandwidth to complete this in that time frame unless you take something else off my plate" (WORK-LIFE HARMONY). Perhaps you need to tell a team member those jokes they are making aren't funny and could be really offensive to others on the team (BELONGING).

Maybe you hold the belief that you'll look weak if you ask for help, but that is false; knowing what you need and seeking it out in productive ways is a strength. Maybe you think, "I can't depend on others." While it's true that you can't depend on everyone all the time, if you have the "go it alone" mindset, your motives will most likely suffer. Sometimes you need to give others the benefit of the doubt and not assume things. Maybe they will understand and help, maybe they will at least be a bit more receptive, or perhaps they won't get it or say no, but you won't know if you don't try. You have to be willing to deal with icky situations at times to eventually get to the other side.

I can't tell you your courageous communication will always be well received by other people. What I do know is you can't hold these limiting beliefs and also get the assistance you need from others to get your motives met. You have to choose. Your well-being is more important, and most often being a brave communicator will serve you, and it will also inspire others to be brave too.

3. EMBRACE HEALTHY CONFLICT

"If you avoid conflict to keep the peace, you start a war inside yourself."
—Cheryl Richardson

We all have our own threshold for discomfort around conflict, but conflict avoidance is all too common. Often, we dodge conflict because either we don't want to feel bad or we don't want someone else to feel bad. The irony is, more bad comes from not dealing with conflict head-on, from not being open and honest. What would it look like to work somewhere where people were radically candid with one another when it comes to their needs? Where it was the norm and not the exception?

The idea behind radical candor, as explained in Kim Scott's book *Radical Candor: Be a Kick-Ass Boss Without Losing Your Humanity*, is that you care personally and challenge directly.[4] She has said compassionate candor would be more accurate, but "radical" gave it the edge she felt it needed at the time. Hitting on the necessary component of "compassionate" with your candor resonates with me because it speaks to the importance of saying what you think and being honest while having good intentions and caring about and respecting the person you are saying it to.

If you believe unnecessary risk is being taken by not following certain protocols (SECURITY), then you need to speak up. If you are having an issue with someone, you should talk to them instead of gossiping behind their back (PEER CONNECTION). If you discover you are making less money than another work peer in the same role, you need to address this with your boss (FAIRNESS).

You have to learn to invite rather than shy away from hard conversations, and you need to handle it well when you are on the receiving end of someone communicating in a compassionately candid way with you about motives. You may hear things you disagree with or feedback that's hard and hurts your ego. Invite the honesty from others, but don't react defensively or let your emotions take you on a roller coaster. There is a lot of value in healthy, constructive conflict; find the value in it.

COURAGEOUS COMMUNICATION IN ACTION

The more you model being a courageous communicator with others and ask them to do the same with you, the better off you will be. Let me give you an example of courageous communication in action. At one point I was having difficulty with someone on my team whom I'll call Adam. Adam joined our team knowing he was sacrificing some of his WORK-LIFE HARMONY to take on our work alongside his other business. But he felt good about this, given the holistic health of his other four motives—VARIETY, INNOVATION, PASSION, and FUN—getting a major boost. He had a lot of PASSION for our mission, it would add more VARIETY to his work, it could scratch his itch for greater INNOVATION, and he would have some FUN while doing it.

However, over time, his PASSION and INNOVATION started to collide with my need for ACHIEVEMENT and to reach our goals. Rather than focusing on brand objectives, his work was driven by his wanting to push the envelope with ideas that weren't a good fit for us, nor that we had budget for. He was ignoring some simple tasks that needed to be done in favor of more FUN passionate projects. I noticed his PASSION start to extinguish and engagement go down. I reached out to him to have a conversation about this.

Given I knew WORK-LIFE HARMONY was one of his motives and I had a sense he was struggling more than anticipated, I asked him how he felt about it. He said not only was his WORK-LIFE HARMONY motive struggling but it was now so low that it was harming his four other motives, too. With the pressure to get the work done quickly, he felt less PASSION and FUN and more stress. He also shared that he didn't want to let me down, that he respected and knew how hard I was working toward my goals for ACHIEVE-MENT and dreams for Motives Met FUTURE SUCCESS. And he knew my WORK-LIFE HARMONY wasn't strong either, even though it wasn't a top need for me.

I also was able to share where I was struggling with my motives and how he was impacting them. Having this understanding from one another then provided a productive way forward to problem-solve with actions like determining where we could bring in a freelancer for the smaller work to free up more of his time. I also said that I would need him to commit wholeheartedly to the projects and deliverable times he did agree to take on, while we outsourced the others. He agreed he needed to be better at being realistic with timelines and not overpromising, which then left me in a tough spot to pick up the slack.

We also talked about how to find alignment between out-of-the-box thinking and creativity while also needing to honor the business side of things. Small things like starting with the objectives and criteria for evaluating work at the beginning of the meeting would ground us in how we were evaluating the work instead of letting personal preferences dictate decisions. I needed to honor his creative process and understand that it was part of him meeting his motives, but he also had to honor our goals.

I won't tell you these conversations are easy or fun, but they are easier when you have motives to guide you, less painful if even one person has the mindset and vocabulary, and far less painful if both people or all the people in the conversation have the shared mindset and vocabulary.

YOU CAN LEAD IMPORTANT MOTIVE CONVOS

What happens when people you work with don't have the motive knowledge you do and you need to have a tough conversation? While shared motive understanding makes these conversations easier, it's not necessary that the other person have the knowledge for you to have the conversation; you can lead them with your own knowledge.

I'll use my friend Gabe's situation as an example. After he took the assessment, Gabe told me about a coworker who was really killing Gabe's PEER CONNECTION motive. On their weekly virtual team meetings, Rachel would constantly jab at Gabe. He was the new, hungry sales guy, young and eager, whereas she had been at the company twenty years and didn't want anything to change, didn't like the kudos he was getting or new ideas he brought. She wasn't particularly nice to anyone, he said, except the three people on the team she was good friends with, but she particularly bullied Gabe and put him down in front of the team and even made comments about his personal life based on what she saw on his Instagram. These three friends would be visibly texting one another over the virtual meeting and laughing; it was pretty obvious they were talking about their coworkers. And the boss? Well, he didn't like conflict. Sometimes he would throw out a "be nice" comment if someone was jabbing, but he let this dynamic continue.

Gabe's PEER CONNECTION motive was suffering, and after he talked about it with me, he decided he absolutely had to address this. He sent Rachel a note on their messaging app to see if she could chat for a few minutes. When they got on the phone, he said to her, "I think being an honest and open communicator is always the best approach with others, so I wanted to come to you directly and see if there is something I've done to upset you in some way, because I get the sense that you have an issue with me." But Rachel denied having an issue with him. She said she had no idea what he was talking about. Then he said, "I hope if there is an issue that you will discuss it with me. I know you are the seasoned person on our team and I am new, but I'm not going to tolerate being put down in meetings or talked about. I came from a great team at my last job, and it's important to me to have good connections at work. It's a big contributor or detractor from my well-being. I hope things can change moving forward."

That was not an easy conversation to have, but man, was it worth it. Rachel didn't start going out of her way to be friends or particularly nice, but Gabe told me she did stop picking on him in meetings, her demeanor changed, she was much more pleasant, and it opened up his ability to connect more with others on the team.

Having conversations about your motives can be easy or at times tough, but it is an important gateway to strengthening your motives. Even if the other person doesn't share the language you now have, you can still guide the conversation with your own knowledge. You have validated results to explain why something matters to you, and you can use that as a lead-in to talk to your boss, for example, about the motives that are met and the ones that you need their support on.

PUTTING INSIGHTS INTO ACTION
START TALKING!

- Think about a relationship in your work life you would like to improve. What are a few questions you might want to ask this person about their needs at work that would be valuable?

- What might be an easy or interesting way to get a conversation going around a specific motive or two on your team?

- What parts of your motive story did you decide in the last chapter would be helpful to share with others? Determine the next steps to share with people that would benefit you.

COMMIT TO BEING A COURAGEOUS
MOTIVE COMMUNICATOR

I want you to commit to being a courageous motive communicator at work. If you already are, I want you to solidify your commitment. Start thinking about where it would benefit you most to be more vulnerable with motives, ask for what you need, and embrace healthy conflict. Who in particular would you need to have courageous conversations with to strengthen your motives? In the next and final step on the pathway, you will incorporate these conversations into your Work Life Well-Lived Action Plan.

MEET MOTIVES

UNDERSTAND BE MINDFUL EVALUATE COMMUNICATE MEET MOTIVES

CHAPTER 11

PRIORITIZING YOUR HEALTH AND HAPPINESS AT WORK . . . *REALLY* PRIORITIZING IT

The fifth and final step down the Motives Met Pathway is to *MEET MOTIVES*—to take the actions, make the changes, celebrate where you are, and evolve.

Here is where you take all those insights, solidify your Work Life Well-Lived Action Plan, and commit to that action plan, making well-being a true priority. This brings me to the last of our dream killers.

Dream Killer #10:
We don't prioritize health and happiness at work enough.

Now this may seem a bit odd for me to bring up at this point, if you have picked up this book and made it this far. You are all in on the importance of work health and happiness, right? That may be true, and hopefully if I have done a good job, it is.

But I need to drive this point home because historically for too many, well-being at work hasn't been a priority for themselves or other people. That was certainly true for me, and I don't want that to be the case for you—now or in the future. I don't want you to slip into old patterns of excuses or pulling back from your priorities. A common culprit standing in the way of your work health and happiness is that it just doesn't make it to the top of the list. That even if you believe health and happiness matter, if you evaluated your actions rather than your words, they wouldn't align and show this to be a top priority.

In the past, have you lived the steps on the Motives Met Pathway? What tools have you used, how much time have you carved out, how many steps have you taken to enhance, assess, and reflect on your human needs at work? Have you tended to your work relationships with care and supported others' top needs the way you want yours to be supported?

Even for those of us who fully believe in the importance of thriving at work, the other demands in life and the busyness can be enough to veer us away. If work well-being can take a back seat for advocates, imagine how it can fall to the wayside for skeptics!

Perhaps finances, or specifically being the breadwinner for your family, leaves you feeling obligated to stay where you are, without the ability to demand more from your job or leave if you're unhappy. This was true for my friend John, a medical sales representative who sent me a note on LinkedIn after I posted a podcast interview. He wrote, "I just left a job where I was highly thought of and had built a great network because of poor quality of life and lack of leadership support. I was also unfortunately known as the 'workaholic.' It was an extremely hard decision to make as a father and family provider to walk away, but I was extremely unhappy and it was taking a serious toll on me, and I realized for my family too. I wasn't showing up as the father and husband I wanted to be. Thank you for the work you are doing to normalize prioritizing your mental health and happiness at work and that just because you have a 'good' job doesn't mean the healthy choice is to stay. Motives Met really reinforced that for me."[1]

It can be tough to walk away from a job unless you have another one lined up, and if you would be taking a financial cut, that adds to the pressure to stay where you are. My mom felt that pressure. She was the only income for three kids for many years; and while she had more than one job offer to move from the agency to the client side, where her needs would be healthier, she would have taken a big pay cut, which she felt she couldn't do. Today she wishes she had chosen differently and sacrificed some pay to get her motives met.

I won't be the one to tell you that if your well-being and mental health are poor, the answer is to simply quit today! There are many factors to consider, but what I will tell you, and what I believe you also know in your heart by now, is that not having your motives met will eat away at you. And that's not sustainable.

You need to prioritize making your motives healthy and know you are worthy of the pursuit of having them flourish. If that isn't possible in your current job, in your current life, then this chapter is where you take the first step forward and then the next, toward making that possible. Quitting tomorrow may in fact be exactly what becomes part of your Work Life Well-Lived Action Plan; or it may eventually be when it's the right time. If and when that time comes to leave your job, you now have the wisdom to know what you need to look for in a new job, and how to ask good questions in the interview to determine if your most important motives will be met there. There is also a lot you can do in your current job or career path to strengthen motives. The grass isn't always greener, but whether you stay or go, prioritizing your health and happiness at work is a must.

WHAT IF YOU FEEL STUCK?

It may not be finances that lead you to stay in a job that's not fulfilling your needs. It could be what I call the guilt factor. You might think other people have it worse than you do, so you shouldn't complain. Or you have a nice job title or make a decent salary to support your family, so you should just be grateful and get on with it. Or perhaps this is the job you had wanted for years—so why would you be unhappy?

I have heard so many people stuck in this mindset, particularly older generations who weren't brought up with the same deserving beliefs that Gen Zers have, for example. A sense of being stuck can also stem from self-imposed fears and negative thinking patterns, worries you can't make your business work, doubt you will get a better job, or hopelessness that there isn't anything you can do in your current situation to make things improve.

There is still the old adage that lingers in some people's minds that yeah, work is going to kinda suck, and that's just the way it is. You can get tunnel vision—and that's what happened to me when I was working at that toxic company. My coworkers and I were all in the trenches of misery together, and it was just normalized to us that this was our environment, so we needed to accept it and deal with it.

There is also the "one day . . ." thinking. *One day, once I've slaved enough, have a certain level of experience, or have reached a certain job title, only then will I have the luxury to prioritize my wants and needs at work. But I can't prioritize them now.*

So many of the beliefs that drive us are unconscious, invisible. Our "unconscious commitments" end up taking precedence over our "conscious commitments." Consciously, you may be committed to setting boundaries with yourself to honor your WORK-LIFE HARMONY, but unconsciously you are committed to saying yes to everything to prove your worth. Consciously, you are committed to delaying gratification and putting in the work now to have the long-term career and FUTURE SUCCESS you want. But unconsciously you are committed to having more free time now. Consciously, you are committed to speaking up if your FAIRNESS motive is compromised and you are passed up for a promotion because you are a woman, but unconsciously you are committed to comfort and avoiding conflict.

If you had asked me at that rock-bottom point in my work life if my well-being mattered, I wouldn't have said no it doesn't. I consciously would have said of course it does. But deep down I didn't believe that it did, or really that it could. I hoped one day it would matter, but today wasn't that day. Our unconscious commitments can be stronger than our conscious ones because we don't have the awareness around them.

When you think about our Dream Killers, it makes sense that well-being at work hasn't always gotten the commitment it deserves.

If you assess your past behavior, it might not represent true commitment to creating your best work life, but the past does not need to be the future. With the right mindset about motives, including more wisdom around what you need for your greatest well-being now and in the future, you can truly commit to creating a work life you want to wake up to every day.

Before you start creating your Work Life Well-Lived Action Plan, I want to share a bit more about how to think about and approach meeting your motives and supporting others' motives. **Let's start with the fact that meeting motives happens in two places: thought and action.**

THOUGHT

"Thought is action in rehearsal."   **—Sigmund Freud**

Anything you want to do, change, or become starts in your brain first. When thinking about desired outcomes in life, we tend to focus on behaviors, but your thoughts create your feelings, your feelings fuel your actions, and those actions determine your outcomes. How you simply think about one of your motives—the meaning you give it, the thoughts around the changes you want to make or goals you have related to it—are everything. Even with all of the tools, managing our human brains can be difficult. Writing this book, for example, was a main part of my action plan for my FUTURE SUCCESS motive. I outlined the steps to take to make it happen, and the actions were clear.

Now don't get me wrong, those actions were hard, harder than I ever could have imagined—so many hours of writing, countless late nights and weekends. But if you weren't reading the pages of this book right now, it wouldn't have been because of the difficulty of those actions but because of all the thoughts in my brain that almost stopped me from doing the actions. "You aren't a good enough writer; this is too hard." "Maybe it's better to write the book later when you have more time." These underlying thoughts and beliefs could have gotten the best of me, but I worked on my mindset.

Do you need to work on your mindset with some of your motives? Do you need to change limiting beliefs? Do you need WORK-LIFE HARMONY but tie your self-worth to being the hardest- and longest-working person in your company? Do you desire SELF-ESTEEM but believe you shouldn't put your ideas out there because you are the least experienced on the team? Do you want to have GROWTH in a new area of your career but tell yourself it will be too hard and take too long for it to happen?

ACTION

"Sometimes what you don't do is just as important as what you do."

—Greg McKeown

Once you get your mind in the right place, what actions do you need to take? If you own your own business and thrive using your PERSONAL STRENGTHS but find yourself spending the most time on your areas of weakness, should you consider hiring someone or outsourcing those tasks? If you need CLEAR EXPECTATIONS to be successful and they are lacking, can you put together a document with what you perceive your responsibilities and role to be and questions you have to review with your boss for greater clarity?

Meeting your motives is about both what you do and what you *don't* do. It's often saying no in order to say yes to your most important needs in order to stay aligned with what matters. It's saying some of the following: "I'm no longer taking on clients with work I'm not passionate about" (PASSION). "I'm not going to stay silent when I don't agree" (FREE EXPRESSION). "I'm not going to stifle my fun spirit to 'be more professional'" (FUN). "I'm saying no to taking a job that offers me more money, but the stress will be incredibly high" (CALMNESS). "I'm saying no to doing things the same way they have always been done" (INNOVATION).

MEETING MOTIVES MEANS CONTROLLING THE CONTROLLABLES

"You only have control over three things in your life—the thoughts you think, the images you visualize, and the actions you take."

—Jack Canfield

Identify the things that matter, determine what is in your control related to what matters, and focus there. Sounds simple, but these wild human brains of ours just love to focus on things outside of our control. Remember that your attention is the most precious resource in your life. Don't waste that precious energy ruminating, stressing, and wishing on things that are outside your sphere of influence. Venting every day about the people you work with who you don't like (PEER CONNECTION), hoping that the time will magically appear for you to get the degree (GROWTH), being constantly frustrated your manager is too busy to help (MANAGER SUPPORT)—these things will *not* strengthen your motives. It can even help to do a mental exercise or use a piece of paper to look at your current circumstance and separate out what's within your control and what's not.

MEETING MOTIVES IS ABOUT TAKING BIG OR DIFFICULT STEPS

"Be willing to be uncomfortable. Be comfortable being uncomfortable. It may get tough, but it's a small price to pay for living a dream."

—Peter McWilliams

Investing the money. Taking the risk. Changing that belief system. Putting in a lot of time. Having that hard conversation. Setting that tough boundary. Asking for big favors.

Meeting your motives can mean big things, more difficult things. This means you have to grow your tolerance for discomfort and have resilience. Quitting your job to pursue your PURPOSE or standing up for what is right when your FAIRNESS is being threatened with discrimination can feel good but also *not* so good. It can feel scary or worrisome. We talked about the emotional experience behind our needs. When your motives are met, you feel the desired emotions you want to feel. But to get to that place you may have to be willing to feel even more discomfort now to get to the other side. At times big changes can be exciting and feel easy and at times they won't, but meeting your motives is about both big and small actions, easy and difficult ones, as well as the "medium" ones in between.

MEETING MOTIVES IS ABOUT TAKING SMALL OR SIMPLE STEPS

"Small seemingly insignificant steps completed consistently over time will create a radical difference."   **—Darren Hardy**

There's the saying that the small things can be the big things, and that is absolutely true. Supporting motives can be the small yet significant things you do. Your microchanges, tiny actions, and habits matter; you want to "think big" and "think small." Bigger leaps can be more difficult, so we can sometimes limit ourselves by thinking that's the only way to make progress. As a result we never even get started in the right direction. The small steps are the catalyst to the bigger results.

Making big commitments on small things can make a difference for your motives. It's making a conscious effort to switch up tasks throughout the day (VARIETY). It's trying on new software systems or learning new AI technology to see where you can create efficiencies to save more time (BALANCED PACE). It's carving out fifteen minutes in the morning with your coffee to read the latest industry articles (GROWTH). For my FLEXIBILITY motive, it was simply designing more of my days purposefully, making small changes to my existing schedule and morning routine.

MEETING MOTIVES IS ABOUT GETTING HELP FROM OTHERS

"When we seek help, people are there to help. But you have to take the first step and ask for it."   **—Angie Ridings**

As you know, you can't go it alone. But when we look at the things we want in life, our brains usually jump straight to *how*: How can I go about doing this? What do I need to do to meet my motives? The incredibly overlooked question we need to also be asking is "*Who* can help me meet my motives?" This mindset shift from "how" to "who" comes from the book *Who Not How* by Dan Sullivan and Dr. Benjamin Hardy. When you find your "whos" to support you, you have their expertise, connections, strengths, resources, perspective, help, and advice, and it opens up all sorts of possibilities. So ask yourself, who do I need and want to seek support from? It can be easy to focus on how, especially for high achievers and perfectionist seekers, something I have certainly struggled with.

I always jump to how to tackle something myself, figure it out, and do whatever needs to be done. This has served me well for sure, but it can also be a downfall. Particularly with PRESTIGE being one of my top motives today, I needed help to grow Motives Met to create a company I am proud of, and as tasks and goals arose, I started shifting my brain to who: Who could help me do this better, with a different perspective or more influence than I have? Who would have sound advice, someone who has been through this before, instead of spending hours trying to figure it out myself?

I cannot even begin to tell you the enormous difference that shift made and will continue to make for my motives and my life. You must identify the people who can help you meet your motives. If you work from home but are craving PEER CONNECTION, is there a mastermind group of like-minded people you could join, or are there friends or work peers in the same location that you could meet up with for a coffee or lunch break once a week? If you want to CHALLENGE yourself, whether it's through learning a new skill or starting a whole business, can you find a mentor? Can you offer to take someone out to dinner who knows what you want to know and get advice?

The "who" is also about identifying who is hindering or harming your motives. Who do you need to approach with compassionate candor and have a less comfortable conversation with, like we talked about on the *COMMUNICATE* step? If you are craving more AUTONOMY, ask your boss if you can have greater empowerment over your work and explain how it will benefit both you and them. If someone is taking credit for your ideas and undervaluing you, tell them it is not okay and your PEER APPRECIATION motive is suffering. If a client is constantly vague about direction but is dissatisfied with your work, articulate that you need CLEAR EXPECTATIONS for this relationship to work well.

MEETING MOTIVES IS ABOUT INVESTIGATING AND EXPLORING

"Exploration is what you do when you don't know what you are doing."

—Neil deGrasse Tyson

At times you might not know what you want to do or should do. That's where you can turn to doing some investigating, researching best practices, reading books, or seeking out information. Someone who is PURPOSE-driven might not be sure about the type of work they want to do that would be more meaningful. Next steps are about exploring potential areas where they have curiosity and interest. If you have the SHARED CULTURE motive and are searching for a new job, take the time to research a company's values, Glassdoor reviews, and explore what current employees say about the culture. If you want your desired ACHIEVEMENT but don't know exactly how to get there, dive into some research or reading to help you figure it out. Sometimes your immediate action is about exploring to figure out the bigger actions you want to take.

MEETING MOTIVES MEANS CELEBRATING AND BEING GRATEFUL

"The more you praise and celebrate your life, the more there is in life to celebrate."   **—Oprah Winfrey**

Sometimes your motives feel really good. You should bask in that and take a moment to acknowledge it, which we don't do enough. Research shows that celebrating "is important to our mental health, self-care, happiness and motivation."[2] Even if your top motives are doing great, your work life very well might not be perfect, and you could still think of a motive that isn't as strong that's not in your top 5.

Our brains have a negativity bias, the tendency I briefly mentioned previously, to focus on the negative and look for the bad stuff because our brains aren't wired for happiness, contentment, or peace; they are wired to keep us alive. Conscious effort is required to overcome this bias and deliberately give weight to good things. Notice that your TRUSTWORTHY LEADERSHIP motive or PEER CONNECTION motive is met, or identify the progress you have made in making them stronger.

If someone has made a significant positive impact on one of your BELONGING or FUN motives, thank them. Share with your manager or company how you appreciate that your need for SECURITY, FREE EXPRESSION, or SHARED CULTURE is thriving. If you reach a motive milestone for your CHALLENGE or ACHIEVEMENT motive, then celebrate big. If your motives are mostly thriving, feel and share the gratitude and joy.

MEETING MOTIVES IS ABOUT PRIORITIZING, ACCEPTING, COMPROMISING

"It's not always rainbows and butterflies, it's compromise that moves us along."   **—Maroon 5**

Even with prioritizing your top 5 out of the 28 motives, you may still have some more prioritizing to do. You may not have the time and resources to accomplish all that you would like to. You may need to accept that one of your motives isn't going to be as strong, that it's worth sacrificing one for the sake of the four others. Acceptance can bring inner peace, relief, calmness, and can even make you experience more useful emotions rather than frustration or stress.

Maybe you are FUTURE SUCCESS driven and you need more WORK-LIFE HARMONY. Those two motives are on opposite sides of the circumplex and can carry tension. It may be difficult for those two things to live in harmony. You may want to make it home for dinner with your family every night, and you may also want to put in the extra work now for bigger payoffs in the future. You could decide you aren't going to make it to the dinner table every night, but you will two nights a week. Or you may decide your bigger goals will need to be less of a priority right now and you will be at the dinner table every night. But whatever you decide, you are doing it purposefully and you can accept whatever the compromise may be rather than beating yourself up. You have laid out clear priorities that you can honor, and that inner turmoil and cognitive dissonance can disappear. You accept the imperfection that brings you peace and honors the complexity of your competing motives.

PUTTING GOOD INTO THE WORLD

We get back what we put into the world. By now, you know or have a greater understanding of the motives of some of the people you work with and of ways to support all of these human needs at work. In the same way you have your "whos" for your motives, you are other people's "who."

Helping to support other people's motives includes all the same things: It can be big and small actions, a simple mindset shift, or helping them celebrate. Remember, it could also be about something you will no longer do, not standing in the way of someone's motive being strong, and not being part of hurting it. As part of your Work Life Well-Lived Action Plan, there is a section for you to think about how you can be a contributor to a thriving culture at work. Especially in today's remote world, we need to be more mindful to support motives and take intentional action.

CHAPTER 12

CREATING YOUR WORK LIFE WELL-LIVED ACTION PLAN

N ow is the time to take all the insights and all the actions you have done along the pathway and solidify your ultimate Work Life Well-Lived Action Plan.

STEP 1: BRAINSTORM YOUR MEET MOTIVES IDEAS

As you start to brainstorm ideas, you can use your Motives Health Scorecard, Motive Reflection Questions, motive stories, and conversations with others to guide you. We have created an action plan template to help you through this, which I will walk through below. You can also access it online at motivesmet.com/book-resources.

SECTION 1:

Select one of your motives. What did you determine the health of this motive to be (drowning, suffering, coasting, or thriving)?

MOTIVE: **PASSION**	MOTIVE HEALTH: **Suffering**
	Drowning, suffering, coasting, or thriving

Image 12.1

SECTION 2:

Decide if this motive is a change, maintain, or elevate motive.

MOTIVE ACTION AREA

MOTIVE: **PASSION**

Identify which action area this motive falls into:

CHANGE ☑   **MAINTAIN** ☐   **ELEVATE** ☐

Change Motive: motives where you want results that are different from where they are now.

Maintenance Motive: motives that are doing well that you want to simply stay well.

Elevate Motive: motives that are strong, but you have the desire or opportunity to elevate higher.

Image 12.2

SECTION 3:

If this motive is a change or elevate motive, fill out this section.

Potential Actions

Brainstorm ideas that would help elevate the health of your motive. Try not to let fear, self-censorship, or practicality block what you honestly desire or prohibit you from focusing on more aspirational ideas. You can include both "realistic" and "reach" ideas; this list is only for you.

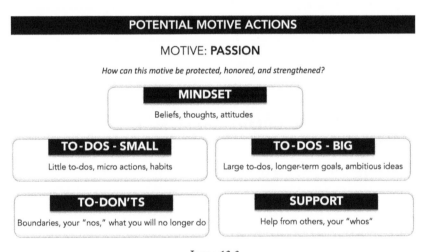

Image 12.3

SECTION 4:

MAINTENANCE MOTIVE

If this motive is a MAINTENANCE motive, fill out this section

What do I need to do to "maintain" the health of this motive? _____

Is there anything that threatens keeping this motive healthy? _____

When should I check back in? _____

Image 12.4

SECTION 5:

What are even one or two things you can do to support other people's motives in your work life?

MOTIVE SUPPORT TO OTHERS

What can I do to help honor, protect, and strengthen motives at work to help others and support a human work world where motives are healthy and ideally thrive? _____

Image 12.5

STEP 2: PRIORITIZE AND FINALIZE YOUR ACTION PLAN

Now comes the tougher part: prioritizing your ideas and finalizing the steps you are going to take. I hate to tell you there is no perfect process for this, but following are the things to consider:

- Impact—What impact will this have on moving me from where I am (current motive rating) to where I want to be (desired motive rating)? Low, medium, high?

- Difficulty level—Is this easy, medium, or hard?

- Resources—What time, energy, money, or support do I have? What time, energy, money, or support do I need? If what I have and what I need aren't in alignment, can I get them in alignment?

- Importance and urgency—Which actions are important and urgent? Which ones seem urgent but are just distractions? Which ones could be delayed?

- Desire—Which ideas/actions excite me the most and the least?

Going through these filters will help you refine your priorities. Make sure you are keeping the following things top of mind:

- You want to focus on controlling the controllables. For example, even if one of your goals is to get a promotion, what steps are within your control there? What actions will set you up for that promotion?

- You will need to make trade-offs and compromises. When you evaluated your motives holistically, did you see friction between motives that you need to resolve?

- Take your big, ambitious ideas and break them into smaller, action-oriented steps.

STEP 3: COMMIT

If you remember, our last and final dream killer was that prioritizing your health and happiness at work can slip through the cracks. Help deepen your commitment by answering the following last few questions:

Commitment questions:

- What benefits will I get if I follow through on my motive action-plan items?

- What can I anticipate might be difficult?

- How will I keep going when things get hard?

- What will it cost me if I don't follow through?

Last but not least, what is the *one* next step you are going to take once you put down this book? Even if that step is just scheduling time on your calendar to create your action plan—a small action. I don't want you to leave this book without specifically identifying the one step you are going to take!

MY WORK LIFE WELL-LIVED

My next step to create my work life that's well-lived is . . .

Image 12.6

PART 3

THE MOTIVES MET PATHWAY FOR LEADERS

CHAPTER 13

LEADING THE WAY TO A MORE HUMAN WORKPLACE

We've just traversed the Motives Met Pathway together, and now we're about to hit it from a leadership perspective. It's time to make a big impact, because for better or worse, our leaders can make or break motives for many. Two of the 28 motives are directly related to the impact that MANAGER SUPPORT and TRUSTWORTHY LEADERSHIP have on the health and happiness of employees. Being a great leader is about coaching, teaching, supporting, serving, and inspiring. It's not about trying to be a therapist. It's not about being perfect. It's not the old-school command and control that no longer works, and never did. And it's not about expecting less than the best from your employees, because performance and reaching goals absolutely matters. To lead people to their best work lives and your best workplace, you need to coach, teach, support, serve, and inspire each person and each team uniquely, based on who they are and the human needs that drive them.

Here in part 3, I will be focusing on people leaders in organizations, but as we all know, being a leader isn't just about a formal title or fancy position. There is information here that will serve you if you want to positively impact others, change your team's micro culture, flex your influence muscles, be a better leader in the future, bring ideas to your company, and be better able to support the dream of a better work world by understanding the organizational side of things. If you want the work world to look different, then you need to advocate for it, and these chapters will help you do that. If you aren't a formal people leader, I encourage you to read the parts that interest and benefit you before moving to the book's conclusion in chapter 19.

A DOSE OF INSPIRATION FOR PUTTING PEOPLE FIRST

Legendary Gary Vaynerchuk, aka Gary Vee, is someone who rarely needs an introduction, but if you do, he is a serial entrepreneur, CEO of VaynerMedia, five-time *New York Times* best-selling author, and social media icon who also holds a reputation for attracting top talent and driving killer business results due to his unwavering belief in the power of putting employees at the heart of his organizations.

Vaynerchuk says that the second most important person in his entire organization, above his COO or CFO, is his chief heart officer, Claude Silver. Her responsibility? To help him "create the greatest human organization of all time." Whether you are the manager of a small team or a CEO aiming to rival Gary Vee and give him some competition, adopting this mindset is key.

I'm here to guide you toward that vision in the pages ahead. I assure you that Dream Killer #5, that our humanity can be left behind at work, won't stand a chance.

SHARING THE EMOTIONAL LABOR

We have covered the "individual" and "work peers" part of our co-creation of the well-being model, and leaders make up the third and last part. To create a people-first team or organization where people thrive is not solely your burden to bear. But it rests heavily on your shoulders. As a leader you have a powerful impact on motives that others won't have. You may be a person on the team others look up to as a leader, and you influence norms. As the CEO of the company, you determine goals and resources. As a director, you have hiring and firing power. As a manager, you can implement new ideas and be a proponent for change. You have authority, ability, and responsibility.

You are not just responsible for results; you are responsible for the mental, emotional, and social health of the people who create those results. This responsibility can take an emotional toll. A *Harvard Business Review* article titled "The Emotional Labor of Being a Leader" paints this picture well, saying, "Leaders are expected to attend to employees' mental and physical health and burnout (while also addressing their own), demonstrate bottomless sensitivity and compassion, and provide opportunities for flexibility and remote work—all while managing the bottom line, doing more with less, and overcoming challenges with hiring and retaining talent."[1]

That's a tall order, for sure. And it's true, caring for the health of 28 human needs at work is a huge undertaking. And that is why you need help. What's also true is that even if you wanted to go it alone, it wouldn't work. A top-down approach won't cut it, because at the end of the day, culture is people; it's how people think, how they feel, and what they do.

> You must take ownership, but part of that ownership is actually sharing the emotional labor. Not crumbling under the weight of the responsibility but empowering others to share in it.

You don't have control over how people think, feel, and act when it comes to motives, but you do have influence. You want to use that influence to make it possible for everyone to create together. Your job is to do what is in your power so our dream killers don't win out. Your job is to create the conditions where motives and thus your people can thrive.

In parts 1 and 2 of this book, you took the journey as an individual. As a leader, you must care for your own well-being as a human being with human needs. In this part of the book I will help you take action to support each step in your role as a leader to help others care for their well-being. If you want to have a human work culture, if you want all the benefits we have explored from meeting motives, then you need to walk the Motives Met Pathway yourself to understand, be mindful of, evaluate, communicate, and meet motives, while also leading people to walk it with you.

CREATING SHARED MEANING AROUND WORK WELL-BEING

"The pool of shared meaning is the birthplace of synergy."

—Kerry Patterson

Your first order of business is to share what well-being at work really means. A few of our dream killers are directly linked to the confusion and lack of clarity on what health and happiness at work is all about, what it means to have a human workplace, and how to have a people-first approach. For people to successfully work together toward any goal, they of course need clarity on the goal. Sounds simple, but if creating your best workplace with employee well-being is the goal, have you defined what that means for your team or organization? If you asked each employee, would they have the same answer?

You must create shared meaning around what work well-being is and what it isn't. Per Dream Killer #4, it's not Band-Aids, quick fixes, or perks that lack meaning. It's having 28 healthy and thriving motives where possible.

PERSONALIZING YOUR APPROACH

While sharing the responsibility will greatly lighten your load, you still have some heavy lifting to do. You have to take both an individualistic and a collective approach to meeting motives, based on your unique employees, because well-being is personal.

INDIVIDUALIZED APPROACH

When I first had a team of people reporting to me, I was already perceived as a leader in our company and the main lead on a large account. But overnight, it seemed, I was now truly responsible for a team of people who reported directly to me. Was I given any coaching or tools on how to lead well? Definitely not. I had been in enough leadership groups and roles in my life and read enough books to not suck at it, but I could have been so much better.

All leaders could be so much better if given the support from their organizations to lead to the best of their ability. What I did know was that I wanted my team to feel great about their work life and knew that if I could support their needs, then they would also be more likely to support mine.

About three months into having a person on my team, I would take them out for a nice, long lunch away from the office and ask them how they felt things were going so far. I asked them why they had wanted to take the job in the first place, what they liked and didn't like, and what would make them look forward to going to work every day. In hindsight I was trying to figure out their motives. One person was laser focused on a promotion, and I learned their long-term goal was to work on the client side and be a brand manager one day. This person was in school to get their business degree to help them do that. They wanted client exposure, to sit in on bigger meetings, and to absorb and learn. They may have had the ACHIEVEMENT or GROWTH motives or both.

Someone else who newly reported to me wasn't new to the company, but I was being brought in as the more strategic lead on an account that up until then she had been managing on her own. Her message was loud and clear: She knew everything there was to know about this client's business, and she had worked her butt off the last three years to make sure things ran smoothly, which for the most part they had. I could tell she didn't want to feel like she was now the second string and I was the first string, and that I would micromanage and ruin the good synergy she had built on the account. I told her that I had no intention of trying to "take over," that it was actually a relief, given my workload, that I could count on her.

But I also explained that my boss had expectations for me to grow the account and make the client feel like she had senior support from our team. I explained how I needed to be involved in the strategic planning and bigger in-person client meetings and that I could help her to eventually grow into my role by guiding her. She understood the position I was in and felt good about this solution. AUTONOMY would have been one of her five motives, but I would have loved to have known what the other four were.

Another employee was quite different; they were a people person through and through. They loved the fun atmosphere of agency life, thrived on taking clients out to dinner and building business. The motives FUN and PEER CONNECTION drove them. Taking them out to happy hour, letting them plan client events and be a part of new business pitches, and simply being light-hearted went a long way with them.

Bottom line is, learning this information about my team members changed how I coached, taught, supported, served, and inspired them—and I was far from perfect at that time. The Motives Met Pathway would have been a true gift, but taking this person-centered approach and having some sort of inkling of my team's needs made a big difference. It honors individuality, recognizes that people have unique circumstances, abilities, and challenges, and seeks to address them in a personalized manner.

COLLECTIVE APPROACH

It's important to have both the individual motive lens and an interpersonal lens, evaluating relationship dynamics as well as the needs for a collective group. It's focusing on tackling problems, making choices, and finding solutions that positively impact the entire team or community.

There could be two people on your team, for example, who are needing a CHALLENGE, but that might not ring true for the team at large. You will, of course, want to have individual discussions with those team members and problem-solve if, for example, they feel underchallenged or bored at work. From a team perspective, however, what you might see is that PASSION, PEER APPRECIATION, and TRUSTWORTHY LEADERSHIP are top motives for the team. Then you will want to understand why that's true for them. Are these needs well met? Why or why not? You want to ask questions such as, where do we have good connections on the team among those with similar motives, and where may there be interpersonal conflict in the group based on differing needs? Do we have some of our top motives in the same domain, or are they on opposite ends of the circumplex and thus hold more tension? Which motives do we want to focus on from a team perspective?

The following example is based on two different organizations we have worked with at Motives Met. Combining these two will help me to best illustrate the steps forward on the pathway. I am going to use this case study example throughout the leadership part of the book on each step on the Motives Met Pathway so you can see how this all comes to life.

In the circumplex in image 13.1, you can see the nine motives that are rising to the top for this collective group. In this group dynamic, WORK-LIFE HARMONY was the top motive for sixteen people/50% of the group, who had it in their top 5 motives, with PEER CONNECTION right behind it at fourteen people or 43% of the group.

THE MOTIVES CIRCUMPLEX™

Image 13.1

Teams and organizations find it fun and insightful to discover patterns, similarities, or differences in their unique group circumplex. Some groups can have more diverse motives, and other times a majority of motives fall into the same motive domains. I was working with a new director who had just joined her company, and she said that having insight into her team's top motives painted a picture of a good place for her to start in understanding her team; it was a way to create a team vision for everyone. While all 28 motives need to be supported at work and while you still need to tend to individual employee needs, examining your collective motive helps to provide a focus for a team, company, or community to work toward together.

PUTTING INSIGHTS INTO ACTION
LEAD THE VISION

It's time to introduce the Motives Met Pathway to your employees and give them the foundational understanding to build from.

Choose a good time and setting: To kick off the way forward for well-being with greater inspiration and vivacity, consider having a special team meeting, workshop, or well-being session at your next off-site or company gathering. How can you give it the attention it deserves and not make this feel like some lackluster corporate initiative or a box you are just checking? You can also start using communication channels like Slack or social media, send out a meaningful letter, or even better, a video to employees to help expand the message.

Establish the goal and clarity: Unite people behind the goal to co-create your best workplace where these human needs thrive and thus everyone thrives collectively. This is where you create the shared meaning around what that actually entails and you have the research from this book, the 28 motives, and the framework to help you teach others what health and happiness at work is truly all about.

Explain the "why": You want to amplify the 28 human needs at work because you care about employees and team members as people and want them to care about one another as people (I hope that's true, yeah?!). Start with your why and you will gain greater commitment and excitement. Talk about the benefits that happen when people's motives are met at work. It's also a good time to mention that if things haven't been going so hot, you realize it, you own it, and you want it to change.

Share the "how": Once you have your why, you help employees understand how together you are going to create your best workplace using the Motives Met Pathway. This isn't pretending you have it all figured out. You don't yet know all the details of the "how" for all the motives in your workplace, *but* you have a path, and you are going to figure out the how together as you take each step.

Reinforce the "who": Everybody. This is on everyone! I will talk more about setting the expectation for "motive mindfulness" for each employee in the next chapter, but reinforce that you want to hear ideas, concerns, and inputs from employees throughout this journey; be sure to provide an easy avenue for them to give you that feedback.

CHAPTER 14

CO-CREATING A CULTURE OF WELL-BEING

A s a leader you have a lot going on, so historically maybe—
just maybe—you've been taking a bit of a laid-back or
reactive approach to employee health and happiness. I
mean, we all fall into that trap sometimes, right? Assuming things
will sort themselves out without putting in the intentional effort?

Leaders also fall victim to Dream Killer #6, that the default mode
can be passive and reactionary rather than purposeful even if you
don't mean for it to be. We all can be on autopilot when it comes
to being mindful of our own needs. It's also easy to be on autopilot
when it comes to leading the health of these needs. Maybe you didn't
realize you needed to do something different until multiple people
on your team left. Or you received feedback about motive areas that
were unfavorable, and you knew you needed to fix something. Maybe
you've seen productivity and satisfaction go down and burnout and
disengagement go up.

Given there is (thankfully) so much buzz around this topic, you might have realized a people-first workplace is something you should focus on. Whatever the case, you picked up this book for a reason. You have the right intentions paired with new knowledge, and that knowledge is now power for you to lead with motives in mind using the three A's—conscious *awareness*, focused *attention*, and intentional *action*. And you're ready to have your employees take that mindful approach alongside you.

TAKING A LOOK IN THE MIRROR

It's time to get real with yourself. The place to start is going inward. Are you modeling mindful motive behavior? Have you ever asked people how they feel about the events or efforts you have in place to bring FUN into work? Or do you assume everyone finds them enjoyable and do the same things on repeat? Do you make everyone feel seen and important, that they matter, whether they are the intern, the new employee, or the "lowest-level" person (SELF-ESTEEM)? Do you dump your worries on others in unhealthy ways that make them unnecessarily worry and feel insecure (SECURITY)?

Do you refer to your team or company as a "family," which can make employees feel pressure to put up with toxic behaviors for the sake of family loyalty (SHARED CULTURE)? How do you react if employees give you feedback or share their disagreements and concerns (FREE EXPRESSION)? Are you taking your vacation and unplugging to set a good example, or are you working the whole time (WORK-LIFE HARMONY)? Bottom line, thinking about Dream Killer #7, that we struggle to support motives in a meaningful way, where are you personally helping motives and where are you harming them?

ARE YOU EMBRACING MOTIVE DIVERSITY?

When you aren't inclusive and mindful of others' motives, you can lose good people for no good reason, no matter the industry, whether it's hospitality, health care, or technology. Andy, a young go-getter working in the cannabis industry in San Francisco, needed to be challenged to feel like he was growing to reach his full future potential to flourish at work. (PASSION, GROWTH, CHALLENGE, FUTURE SUCCESS, and CLEAR EXPECTATIONS are his core motives.)

He worked for a manager who didn't know this about him and was motivated differently. Andy's boss loved the people in the cannabis industry, and his motives were about the community of like-minded people, the culture, and having fun at work. This was not to say that Andy didn't also appreciate these motives, but they were not his top priorities. The two seemed to have very different needs.

The disconnect is this: **We often tend to operate under the assumption that others require what we require, that others feel how we feel**. Andy was doing well, he was a top seller on the retail floor and had built up a relationship with many repeat customers, including the president of one of the top tech companies in downtown San Francisco who would ask for Andy personally when he came in. Andy tried more than once to approach his boss and explain what his goals were, seeking advice on how he could prove himself and get to the next level, but his boss just sort of brushed him off, told him to relax and have fun, to not worry about the future so much and that he was doing great and would get there in time. The boss didn't have bad intentions, but he was dismissing Andy's needs.

If Andy's manager didn't give him the opportunity to try new things, expand into more meaningful work, and show Andy what he felt he was capable of achieving, Andy would be likely to leave—and in fact, that's exactly what happened. Andy left and went to another cannabis dispensary where he was given the chance to grow. There, management coached him on the small areas he could improve upon, taught him some new things, and then he was promoted until he worked his way up from a retail associate to a top brand buyer. Andy's previous company lost out on a valuable employee, one who was their top seller. You can guess where Andy's client, the president of that top tech company, took his business when Andy left.

MOTIVE JUDGMENT

It's detrimental when leaders place unfair judgment on motives. Research shows that managers misjudge people by believing that those who are not "calling-oriented" lack the same performance and commitment as those who say they are. A friend in HR shared with me that her CEO was upset when he found out one of their employees had a side business on Etsy, which, she told the team, was going well. She had to break it to him that not everyone felt the same PURPOSE within the company as he did, given it was his company!

This employee was not an underperformer at the company. If she found meaning in the creative Etsy outlet and gained additional profits from that business, that was something the employer should support. And man, was she right! An employee may need FUN or FLEXIBILITY to be most fulfilled at work, not PURPOSE, but it doesn't mean they aren't just as successful or dedicated.

MOTIVE NEGLECT

A manager had an aha moment with his team when he realized his tendency toward AUTONOMY and CHALLENGE wasn't helping one of his team members who needed CLEAR EXPECTATIONS. After our workshop with his team, he shared with me, "I didn't think these things were unimportant, I just wasn't paying attention to them." Part of the appeal for this manager joining the startup was that he would be able to carve his own path; the company had general but loose goals. He was challenged to figure out where the company was going a day at a time and originally had no one to manage.

His employee was frustrated because she felt he wanted her to read his mind. He wouldn't provide clarity around the work and expectations, and then wouldn't always be satisfied with the work she did. He realized his lack of attention to provide clarity on what success looked like wasn't helping either of them, and that while he might thrive with looser guidelines, that wouldn't be true for everyone.

It's easy for motive diversity to be put to the wayside unintentionally, but with the Motives Met Pathway you have greater awareness of how you can be more inclusive, empathetic, and mindful toward all motives.

BUILD SHARED COMMITMENT AND HOLD PEOPLE ACCOUNTABLE

"Individual commitment to a group effort—that is what makes a team work, a company work, a society work, a civilization work."

—Vince Lombardi

Now that everyone knows that honoring, protecting, and strengthening motives is the way to well-being, you must inspire a collective commitment to actually doing it. There's no room for half-hearted efforts; you need everyone to wholeheartedly commit to giving a damn if you want to make a real impact. Set the expectation that each person is responsible for showing up in meaningful ways to support their own top motives and the motives of others. This goal means developing a unified belief system that everyone deserves healthy motives, while being authentic in saying it doesn't mean everybody will love one another all the time.

Creating a dynamic where people care, where goodwill is at the heart of how people show up, really matters. James Rhee, goodwill strategist and entrepreneur, shared this in his TED talk "The Value of Kindness at Work": "Kindness distributes the joy of problem solving to everyone. It creates a safe environment that unleashes innovation, especially the unselfish kind."[1] Kindness can be sorely underestimated at work. In a study analyzing more than 3,500 business units with more than 50,000 individuals, researchers found that acts of courtesy, helping, and praise were related to core goals of organizations. Higher rates of these behaviors were predictive of productivity, efficiency, and lower turnover rates.[2]

When employees show care, notice it. Celebrate it. Reward it. Have people share the ways others support their motives. Use the degree to which people uplift these vital human needs at work as promotion criteria; if they don't support the motives people need most, should they really be promoted to a position where they lead more people? On the other side, if they elevate motives and could lead others on the pathway, that's exactly the type of people leader you want, right?

So how about when employees don't show care? Well, don't look the other way! If someone isn't living your company values (unmet SHARED CULTURE), if they are barking orders at people and telling them what to do (unmet AUTONOMY), if they constantly talk over people in meetings and dismiss them (unmet FREE EXPRESSION), then you need to hold them accountable. Here's something else: The same goes for clients, customers, and partners. If they are harming motives, you have to hold them accountable, too. Doing this is not fun. It doesn't make you more popular or likeable. These conversations addressing behavior aren't comfortable, and that is why lack of accountability runs rampant at work. Some leaders will hide behind the idea that they don't want to make people feel bad, but the truth is *they* just don't want to feel bad. The employees who don't show care, the people who consistently harm motives will turn any chance of a culture of well-being into ill-being. Those people have no business working for you or with you. As Gary Vee says, "Focus on people that show humanity. Remember, A+ human beings with B- skills always beat A+ talent with C- personality."[3]

There are some who won't love being accountable to a new standard of thinking, feeling, and behaving. If you lead other leaders, managers, or supervisors, this could be a big shift in what you are expecting of them, and some may want to rise to the challenge while others may not be as thrilled. Employees often don't like feeling powerless to effect change, which can lead to feelings of victimization. But many people will gladly rally behind this change as the new responsibilities empower them. Another benefit? It helps employees have compassion for you.

One of the leaders we worked with shared this after using the Motives Met Pathway with his employees: "I really felt a newfound sense of unity. People could see how tough it is to get all of these motives in harmony and how they actually had a huge part in that happening. I was able to establish that they could and should expect our leadership to care about these needs at work but that we expected them to care too. We had a few big problems that needed solving, and I owned that truth and my part in it but also made it clear the only way this was going to work is if everyone stepped up. I was told by many people how they felt good about the way forward."

CREATE AN "OTHERISH" CULTURE

What this all ladders up to is creating a culture where:

- People aren't selfish; they're not focused only on their motives.

- People aren't selfless; they don't overextend their time and energy and put others first at the detriment of their own needs.

- People are "otherish"; they strike a balance between their own needs while still caring for others.

This concept comes from Adam Grant, organizational psychologist, Wharton professor, and best-selling author of the book *Give and Take: Why Helping Others Drives Our Success*. He says, "If takers are selfish and failed givers are selfless, successful givers are OTHER-ISH: they care about benefiting others, but they also have ambitious goals for advancing their own interests."[4]

Creating this dynamic manifests in developing a sense of caring, compassion, and respect generally toward all motives. But the three A's really strengthen when in work relationships there is the conscious awareness, focused attention, and intentional actions in knowing the top motives driving each person's work wellness. We already covered this relationship dynamic previously, so I won't belabor this point, but empowering employees to know and discuss their top needs with one another makes working relationships better and an "otherish" culture possible.

As a leader you also need to take this to heart; you are a human being with your own motives that need to be met. Some leaders care too little about others, and other leaders care too little about themselves for the sake of others—and neither is what we are aiming for here. You must meet your motives for your own well-being, which will then put you in a better position to lead others to do the same.

HELPING OTHERS LOOK IN THE MIRROR

Once people are committed, you want to help them look in the mirror and observe themselves. Are they being mindful of motives? Your employees need direction on HOW to show up in meaningful ways. A big factor here we have talked about thus far is respecting motive diversity—being inclusive with motives rather than exclusive. In other words, people have to understand they need to respect needs they may not care much about personally, that it's not just about them but the collective as well.

LIVING IN THE TENSION

Let me paint a picture of how all these pieces come together to create a mindful motive dynamic. A struggle I've discussed with many leaders is around the difficulty in navigating the need for FLEXIBILITY, which can include remote working, and the need for PEER CONNECTION, which can be strengthened by working with people in real life and/or being in an office. It's especially tough given all the noise out there trying to tell people what is the "right answer." On one side is the message and research that shows people want to work remotely, it's the future of work, most people can do their jobs from home with today's technology, and you'll lose your people if you don't. On the other side is data and advice that shows people miss their human-to-human connections at work that can't be replaced over a video call, some work is more effective in person, people often feel isolated and lonely, and remote work can hurt your culture and sense of community. This data says more companies are now realizing this and scaling back on their remote-only approach. These two motives, FLEXIBILITY and PEER CONNECTION, are on opposite sides of the Motives Circumplex for a reason; it's not easy to satisfy both needs.

In the following case study example, you can see this dynamic unfold: 43% of people find PEER CONNECTION to be a top need while 31% find FLEXIBILITY to be a top need. Some people have both of these motives in their top 5 and will experience internal tension. They might desire being able to work from wherever they please while also having the need and desire to have human connection at work, which may be more of a struggle without being in an office or in the same city as fellow coworkers.

Image 14.1

Embracing motive diversity is adopting the collective mindset that the goal is learning to live in the tension of these needs well *and* doing it together. I, for example, have FLEXIBILITY in my top 5 motives, and PEER CONNECTION is not a top motive for me. There will be people like me who are happy to work remotely and don't mind fewer in-office/in-person interactions and even prefer it. I have many different communities I am part of outside of work, so while I am a "people person" who likes to be social, it's not a need I crave as strongly in my work life.

What is also true is that some of the people I work with will need that PEER CONNECTION. A few months ago, I jumped on a video meeting with a newer person who was going to be working with my team moving forward on various projects. I had a ton to do that day and was ready to immediately dive into the task at hand. He seemed to be in a different head space—making small talk and asking me how my weekend was. I was about to say, "It was great; how was yours?" and quickly move on from there, but instead I stopped myself. This person was trying to connect with me, and I knew PEER CONNEC-TION was one of his motives. He was trying to build a relationship, especially given we didn't know one another well yet. Rather than give the short and vague answer, I shared how my weekend actually was and that I had a reunion with some people I had done some hiking trips with. That led us to a whole conversation around shared interest of the outdoors and some of his hobbies as well. Yes, it veered our conversation "off course" for ten minutes, but it was worth it. I could tell he really enjoyed our chat, and you know what, I did too!

The idea is, if I work on a team where some are deeply motivated by human connection, how can I support and have the "otherish" attitude? When a colleague asks if I want to catch up over dinner, even if it isn't a priority for me, could I figure out an evening to get together? If my company is doing an off-site so people can connect in person, even if I would rather be at home, can I show up with a positive attitude and understand the value it adds? Can others also show me the same respect if I am not always up for socializing in the way they want to? Getting people to have this attitude is key, and you having this attitude is also key.

As a leader you have to take a step back and think through aspects of both motives. How can you allow people to work more flexibly? Are there changes that you could make that would make remote work possible or improved? If you do have offices that employees can go to but you find they aren't going, why is that? Is the office built so that people feel there is a purpose in going, or is it full of closed doors and lack of opportunities to connect? Flexibility isn't just about remote work, either. What about flexible work schedules? What about throwing out rigid rules that undermine the freedom of choice?

Switching gears to connection: Would offering coworking spaces be a good option for those who don't want to work from their homes and thrive more being around people during the workday? Could great team or company off-sites be a powerful solution? Does a hybrid model appeal to your employees, or does it not appeal to those who desire FLEXIBILITY because it takes away the option to move away from an expensive city or to work globally? If you are a remote team, what are options to enhance PEER CONNECTION in ways that move the needle? Could you set up a monthly event in different cities to get people together? Give a "connection budget" to each person each month to do something with others in the organization?

There is also the nature of your business to consider. You may have requirements or limitations based on your business that you can't change even though they affect motives.

These are the types of things you have to work through and talk about. To drive home the point once more, do not expect perfection, and make sure your employees understand the imperfect nature of meeting motives as well. Compromise will be essential. Accept that what will work best won't necessarily work for everyone. The truth is, if FLEXIBILITY is a top need and your workplace not only requires everyone to be in the office five days a week but also it is rigid and doesn't give meaningful choices over the who, what, when, where, and how of their work, then this job is not going to be a good fit for FLEXIBILITY-motivated employees; you will lose some of them. If

PEER CONNECTION is a driving need for a person and they feel completely disconnected, never have the opportunity to meet their team members in person, and don't feel a good sense of collaboration, you may lose them.

Yes, you may lose some employees if you can't deliver on supporting their motives, and you have to accept that. The important question you must ask is, could you have kept them? I worked with someone who was an amazing creative designer at our agency who had such PASSION for what he did, I'd bet PASSION would have been one of his top motives. He was promoted to creative director, which meant gone were the days where he would spend most of his time actually creating. Instead, most of his days were spent in meetings, getting on the phone with clients, and managing his team. He voiced his frustrations, but they weren't heard, and he left to start his own freelance business. Did our team need a high-level creative person who would manage and hold the client's hand sometimes? Sure we did. But could they have figured out a way to give him hours back in his day to do what he loved so they didn't lose a beloved and high-performing employee? You bet. On the other hand, if someone on your team finds meaning in teaching, has a PASSION for education, and decides to pursue that by becoming a professor, then cheer them on! For them it's not about the shortcomings of your organization, it's that their PASSION lies elsewhere.

It's not easy, but how do you meet motives on opposite ends of the circumplex? How do you support someone's need to feel valued as an important part of the team (SELF-ESTEEM) while also being able to push them to perform at a higher level so you can meet your own need for pushing boundaries of what's possible (INNOVATION)? How do you support the existing culture and values some of your employees love (SHARED CULTURE) while also expanding to create a workplace where diversity is welcome, along with a new way of being and doing things (BELONGING)?

You can't please everyone all the time, and yet there can be a lot you can do to lessen the friction. You can set yourself up for success by learning to live in the tension well. Accepting the imperfection and messiness of work well-being is the secret to thriving. Where can you problem-solve? Where does there need to be compromise? Where do you have limitations you can't overcome, and where are the ones you can? How do your people really feel? Have you asked what thoughts and ideas employees have? If you ask them, they will come up with all sorts of great ideas to consider.

PUTTING INSIGHTS INTO ACTION
DO A PERSONAL MOTIVE AUDIT

Take some time to reflect. Where have you personally modeled being mindful of motives and where haven't you? You can think of this as a personal audit. Look at the Motives Circumplex and reflect on each motive. Are there some motives you think you do better at supporting than others? Where have you not supported motive diversity? What might need to change? If there are motive areas you are unsure of, ask your employees for feedback!

EMPOWER MOTIVE DISCOVERY

Support your people to discover their top human needs at work. You can use the Motives Met Human Needs Assessment™, as many organizations have resources dedicated to things like culture initiatives, leadership coaching, and team-building that this program could fall into, and I'm happy to say more companies also have budgets specifically dedicated to well-being, mental health, and culture, as they should!

You do not, however, have to use the assessment if that is not a viable option for you. You can talk to your employees about the 28 motives, using the motive summaries and other free resources we provide. Then have each person select the five motives they want to focus on. Those will be their "top 5" that you use for each person as you go through the steps on the Motives Met Pathway. Once everyone takes the assessment (or selects their top 5 to focus on), take some time to absorb the results yourself. Who has what motives? What does your team circumplex look like? Identify the top motives for your group like we shared in our group example. Take some time to digest it before we jump into the next steps.

CHAPTER 15

LEVERAGING MOTIVES ANALYTICS

I f I asked you right now the degree to which your team members have well-being and why, could you articulate that in a meaningful, data-driven way? If an outcome matters enough to invest time and resources to achieve it, it inarguably matters enough to measure it. Per Dream Killer #8, well-being doesn't get evaluated and measured in the way it should, you will miss out on the benefits of having simple well-being analytics if you don't know where the well-being of your employees truly stands. Now that you've used the assessment and established shared meaning around work well-being with your employees, you want to find out how healthy their motives are.

You want a way to measure progress, to see if your efforts are working. You want to catch problems when they are small. You want a fact-based way to obtain budgets or support for things you want to improve. One of the really good things that can happen? You will see what's going great, what's working, what you want to keep doing or do more of; you will see what isn't working, what's at risk, and what needs to change. It's as much about problem finding as it is about problem-solving. Of course, uncovering problems isn't always fun. "I just love hearing about what is going wrong, where people are hurt or struggling, and weak spots"—said no one ever.

DO YOU REALLY WANT TO KNOW?

"If knowledge is power, knowing what we don't know is wisdom."

—Adam Grant

To be able to evaluate well-being well, you have to want to do it. Seems obvious enough, but there can be psychological barriers. Deep down, the way we humans are wired, we don't always want to know the truth; the truth isn't always pretty or easy. We want to know, but we also kinda don't want to know; it's kind of easier not to know. That's truthfully how many leaders and managers can feel. Even when they say they want to hear the truth, a part of them doesn't. This is a normal human response but important to be aware of. In the same way it doesn't feel good to face your lesser met motives, it certainly doesn't feel good for leaders either.

Some leaders are afraid to know. Especially if they can sense things are bad, they are fearful to know just how bad. But this "bad-ness" and its negative effects are happening whether leaders want to admit it or not. A leader can wait until the unfavorable reviews on Glassdoor can no longer be ignored, until the quality of work and profits dwindle, or they lose valuable people; or they can decide to face the issue head-on. Leaders may also feel weighed down by the responsibility. Once they know where the problems are, they can't as easily look the other way and pretend the issues don't exist.

Another fear, the fear of feelings, describes the emotions that may accompany the truths you uncover. You could feel over-whelmed with all the problems, figuring out where to start and what issues to tackle first; helpless because you don't know how to, or feel you can't fix certain problems; hurt by hearing feedback related to your leadership or decision-making; sad that someone isn't happy on your team; annoyed if you don't agree with how someone feels. The fear is often subconscious, but creating a thriv-ing workplace is going to take courage and commitment. You have to want to know the good, the bad, and the ugly. And your people need to believe you really want to know too or they won't be hon-est with you.

It can be easier to want to hear the truth when you believe the truth won't be "that bad," but it's more difficult if you fear more prob-lems coming to the surface. Of course, denial and avoidance won't get you the results you want.

DEVELOPING WELL-BEING ANALYTICS FOR YOUR PEOPLE

Being truly ready and willing to evaluate work well-being is the first step, but then you need to get it right by really listening to your peo-ple. You can listen in group discussions or one-on-one conversations and also listen through data. Here, we want to focus on quantifying the data and developing simple well-being analytics with a survey. Sometimes we are tempted to focus only on things that are easier to measure like absent days or retention rates. Those metrics can absolutely be worth measuring, but they aren't going to shed light on the truth of well-being or where the disease that is infecting it lies. Other times, the temptation is to measure everything you could possibly measure, but then you are in data overload without clear, actionable takeaways. With too many measures, people get distracted, confused, and lose focus of the most important measures.

You need to measure the right things in the right way, and with the 28 motives you now have the ability to do exactly that. I will walk you through five steps to make this as easy as possible for you. In the same way you developed a Motives Health Scorecard for your own motives, you will go through a similar process for your team or organization. I am keeping things basic in this chapter rather than going into the nitty-gritty of survey design—the different scales to use for survey questions and analysis—to not overwhelm you or make this chapter overly long.

The details and template for the survey are provided for you at motivesmet.com/book-resources. Using our template, you can create the survey in an online simple survey builder like SurveyMonkey, Google Forms, Qualtrics, or Typeform. There are also great freelancing platforms like Upwork or Freelancer.com where you can find a freelancer for a low hourly rate to help you. You of course also may have internal tools or people who would handle sending out this survey for you.

STEP 1: MEASURE MOTIVES BY SURVEY

Surveys can get a bad rap for good reason. If the survey isn't asking the right questions, then it's worthless. If your people don't feel they can be honest and they give false information, a survey can do more harm than good. If the survey is too complex and lengthy to digest and take action on the data, it's unhelpful and a burden. If it's the same type of engagement or workplace survey that keeps circulating for years and no changes ever get made, it's frustrating as hell. All are valid concerns.

But good surveys? They can be a gold mine and a sign you care. That's what you want to make clear, that you are doing this survey because you care about your employees' needs. It's not about you, productivity, or how to get them to work more or be more engaged; it's about employees' motives, happiness, well-being, and how you can better support it. If people do believe you genuinely care and that you will actually do something with the information, then most would be happy to take the time to answer questions.

Design a simple, good survey to send to your employees to measure motives. I am a researcher at heart, so I love an in-depth questionnaire that gets at all sorts of details and nuances, but this is not that survey. This is a survey to allow you to develop your simple Motive Health Scorecard for a few reasons.

- We want this to be easy on everyone, short and quick for employees to take, and with digestible results simple enough that any leader or employee could understand.

- This is meant to be a benchmark to start from; the findings will give you insight into strong versus weak areas, and you can start to discuss these with employees, which we will talk about in the next chapter. If you find, for example, PEER CON-NECTION is struggling, you may decide to dive deeper into this area, have a chat with employees about it, and eventually

do more research or a quick poll to find out which ideas resonate to improve it. The research will be in worthwhile areas you
determine from these initial benchmarks.

- You need metrics that you can track over time. This is a foundation that is easy to measure repeatedly, partially because
of its simple and straightforward nature. You have a tight set of
questions you can ask at least once a year or preferably semi-
annually—and then continue to ask.

Ideally, this survey will be anonymous. The goal is that you create
a dynamic in which people have the psychological safety and trust
to honestly share how they feel, but as we already shared, most organizations don't have this in the way they think they do. To get your
most accurate benchmarks, it's best to keep surveys anonymous. The
kicker is, for it to be anonymous you need to be surveying enough
employees. If you have a smaller group or team, you will need to use
your best judgment. You may feel there is a high enough comfort
level to ask certain questions, but know that you may have to take
the results with a grain of salt. Or you may decide to only ask the
questions we outline below that are less vulnerable when you know
your name is attached to it.

You could also decide to discuss these questions with your smaller
team if that feels best to you, and we will talk more about this on the
next step of the pathway. But if the survey is not going to be anonymous and you plan to share people's results with other leaders or the
team, you should also let them know that up front before they take
the survey.

In your motive survey, you are going to ask six questions:

- Question 1—How Met: How well "met" are each of your top 5 motives for you personally?

- Question 2—Organization Motive Support: The degree to which a motive can be strong can be dependent on several factors, some outside of our control. We want to know to what degree you feel our organization creates the conditions for your motives to thrive.

- Question 3—Strongest Motive: Which of your top 5 motives is the strongest?

- Question 4—Weakest Motive: Which of your top 5 motives has the most room for improvement?

- Question 5—Strongest Organization Support Motive: Which of your top 5 motives does our organization support the best?

- Question 6—Weakest Organization Support Motive: Which of your top 5 motives does our organization provide the weakest support for?

In our online resource, we break down in greater detail the way to ask each of these questions. Questions 3 through 6 are another way to gauge motive health that is more comfortable to answer no matter the size of your group, anonymous or not. Even if anonymous, people may tend to skew in a more positive direction on the first two questions. Why? One reason is because they may be skeptical the survey really is anonymous; and second, there is a positive halo effect that often happens across research in general. People tend to skew more positive in their answers than is the reality. This provides another angle to view the health of motives where you get clarity on ones that are weak.

STEP 2: ANALYZE THE DATA AND IDENTIFY YOUR HEALTH BUCKETS

Once you have the feedback collected, you need to analyze the data. I'll be honest, this isn't exactly a straightforward process. Analytical thinking and playing with your specific data will be required. Most survey builder systems provide simple graphs for you to get an overview of the results, and that may be enough for you to get the insights you need; you can also develop your own charts and report.

Using the answers to the six questions, you will determine how you are segmenting motives into "health buckets" of drowning, surviving, coasting, and thriving. You will evaluate the ratings for questions 1 and 2 for how met motives are and the degree of organization support employees rated each one. You will also consider what percentage of motives were rated as a "top met" motive and a motive that had the most organization support, along with what percentage were rated as the weakest met and got the least organization support. Again, our online resource breaks this down further.

Image 15.1 is an example of how some of the well-being analytics for motives looked from our case study group.

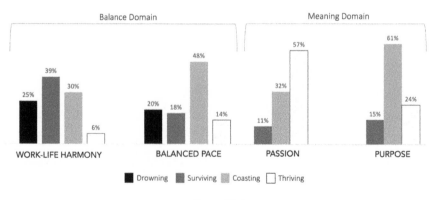

Image 15.1

WORK-LIFE HARMONY is one of the top motives of the group and has 25% of people in the drowning bucket and only 6% in the thriving. PASSION, on the other hand, also a top motive, doesn't have anyone in the drowning bucket, and 57% rated it as thriving. Image 15.2 shows the final health breakdown of the top motives of the group.

MOTIVES HEALTH SCORECARD

MOTIVES		MOTIVE HEALTH
Most important motives for the group		Drowning, suffering, coasting, thriving
MOTIVE 1:	WORK/LIFE HARMONY	Drowning
MOTIVE 2:	PEER CONNECTION	Suffering
MOTIVE 3:	GROWTH	Suffering
MOTIVE 4:	TRUSTWORTHY LEADERSHIP	Suffering
MOTIVE 5:	CALMNESS	Coasting
MOTIVE 6:	INNOVATION	Coasting
MOTIVE 7:	FUTURE SUCCESS	Coasting
MOTIVE 8:	FLEXIBILITY	Thriving
MOTIVE 9:	PASSION	Thriving

Image 15.2

STEP 3: DECIDE HOW YOU FEEL ABOUT YOUR MOTIVE METRICS

With your well-being analytics in hand, how do you feel about what you have discovered? Hopeful? Positive? Disheartened? If your motive health isn't where you want it to be, use this as motivation to spark growth and change. I mentioned that sometimes the whole truth can make you feel a whole lot of things, but now you have a path to guide you to help things improve.

STEP 4: CREATE A SIMPLE REPORT AND SHARE

Take your data and make a short report you can share. Who you share it with and what information you share will be up to you and will depend on certain factors. If, for example, you have a team of fifteen, sharing with everyone the degree to which each person feels their needs are met can be personal information they might not want public. You might instead provide a high-level takeaway you can share with your employees. The story is different in a company of five hundred versus fifty thousand. Use your judgment for what makes sense, but the goal is transparency and to make employees feel you have heard them and you're committed to doing something with this information.

If motives aren't as strong in your culture as you want them to be, then share that and your dedication to improvement. Ask that employees join in their commitment to do their part to elevate motive health as well. You will see on the Leadership *COMMUNI-CATE* step of the pathway how you can use this data to determine motives you want to talk about in greater depth with your team or company. You may choose a few motives that were rated as having the most room for improvement, and ensure you discuss them in a meeting or workshop. Also select a few motives that were strongest to hear more about why.

If you're a manager or HR leader, this information can be helpful to share with your boss. It can at times be difficult to get support to try something new, secure funds, or get something taken off your plate so you have more bandwidth to help support your team in areas they need. If you can show areas that are weak and need attention, you are more likely to get support. If you are a leader with team managers or supervisors in your organization, you will want to debrief them on the insights you learn from their teams.

STEP 5: REEVALUATE

Once you get to the end of the Motives Met Pathway, you will determine the actions you want to take, where you want to invest time, energy, and dollars into creating your best workplace. When you send out this survey again, you will be able to see where you made progress. By reevaluating your motive metrics you can determine the ROI on your investments. You can also build on the survey and ask a few questions related to those investments. How did people feel about them? What seems to be working and what's not?

Use these five steps as a guideline. There are variables you will need to consider for your particular team or company, but to be able to determine the current motive health for employees and the degree they feel your organization supports motives, you will need to evaluate to know current strengths and weaknesses.

PUTTING INSIGHTS INTO ACTION
CREATE YOUR MOTIVE SURVEY

Once employees have taken the assessment, follow up with this short survey you create. You can access our template that outlines the survey at motivesmet.com/book-resources.

Once you get your data back, follow the remaining steps to analyze the data, reflect on how you feel, summarize your findings, and share.

Decide your plan for reevaluation and create a road map for it. It's best to do that now so it doesn't end up getting forgotten. For example, put in your project plans to send the survey out now, and then again six months from now. You may also sync some of your reevaluation check-ins based on your action plan you will develop on the MEET MOTIVES step.

CHAPTER 16

BEGINNING A NEVER-ENDING CONVERSATION AROUND MOTIVES

S ilence will cost you. Do you want someone complaining they aren't happy at work and bringing others down, or do you want them to reflect on why they aren't satisfied and take initiative to seek out ways to be fulfilled? Do you want someone "quiet quitting" and suddenly making life harder on everyone? Or would you prefer they realize this job isn't a good fit, giving you time to make space for a valuable person to come on board? Do you want people on your team being passive-aggressive and lacking collaboration, or would you prefer they have a productive conversation to fix things? Do you want high performers to leave, or should they talk to their manager about what they need?

> Silence is lethal. It will cost you many things—like connection, productivity, and motivation. It will cost you your people.

Remember that research I shared, that 52% of employees exiting their company said something could have been done to keep them, but that conversation never happened? In the three months before their departure, no one talked with them about their fulfillment (or lack thereof) in their job. You don't want this to be your fate.

Sometimes companies will do exit interviews, to talk to employees and understand why they are leaving; most of the time those reasons will be related to unmet motives. But why wait until someone is already leaving and there is nothing you can do about the reasons why they weren't satisfied in their job and at your company? A much better strategy is having conversations with employees *now*. It's having "entry interviews" and "stay interviews." Why did someone want to come work here and take this job, *and* what needs to happen so that they want to stay?

If you don't want Dream Killer #9 (motives are a missing conversation at work) to be a huge roadblock to getting benefits like authentic connection, better relationships, problem-solving, getting and giving support, and the vital insights into how to get your people to want to stay, then you need to be having motive conversations with your employees. You must also guide your employees to reflect and have these conversations with themselves and with each other.

THE TRUTH, THE WHOLE TRUTH, AND NOTHING BUT THE TRUTH

We addressed this in the *EVALUATE* step on the Motives Met Pathway, but I want to reinforce the necessity that as a leader you have to want to know the truth, the whole truth, and nothing but the truth, even if that truth isn't easy or fun to hear. With the well-being analytics on motives, you now have insight into areas of weakness that you will want to discuss with your employees to understand the issues at hand. You will want to talk to people individually and collectively and have them share with you how they feel about their motive health ratings, provide greater insight into why there are problems, and offer solution-oriented ideas. People need to believe you want the good, bad, and ugly. They want to believe they can be honest with you and with one another, and to be able to engage in healthy conflict when needed—or you won't get the truth. You need those vital elements—vulnerability, psychological safety, and trust—to be strong. You must have a culture where courageous communication is not only welcomed but also rewarded and expected.

THE BEDROCK OF PSYCHOLOGICAL SAFETY AND TRUST

Imagine how comfortable you would feel doing the following:

Walk into your boss's office and say . . .

- "You are micromanaging me, and it's really driving me crazy and stressing me out." (AUTONOMY)

- "I don't feel like your direction is clear. You are sending mixed messages and keep changing your mind on what you want, and it's not setting me up for success."(CLEAR EXPECTATIONS)

- "I'm not spending much time doing work I'm passionate about anymore." (PASSION)

- "I need more support and guidance from you but don't feel I am getting it." (MANAGER SUPPORT)

- "Forcing people to attend these 'fun' monthly events is, in fact, not fun for many of us." (FUN)

In a team meeting you say . . .

- "I don't feel like the team appreciates me and recognizes the amount of effort I put in." (PEER APPRECIATION)

- "The people with the most power in the room always dominate the conversation." (FREE EXPRESSION Motive)

- "I feel the quality of work has gone down and our brand image is slipping. We need to make changes." (PRESTIGE)

- "We can say we care about these things, but in actuality we aren't really living what we claim are our values." (SHARED CULTURE)

- "Sending emails and chat messages at all hours of the day and night and expecting me to always be 'online' to answer isn't reasonable." (WORK-LIFE HARMONY)

Even with a whole lot of trust and psychological safety, communicating those things can be tough and feel less than comfy.

Now, imagine a scenario where you have a one-on-one meeting with your boss, a meeting that happens regularly to talk about motives. You know that everyone else on your team is having the same kind of meeting, because this is a normal part of your culture.

Your boss asks you . . .

- "Where do you feel the most freedom and empowerment in your job? Where do you feel the most powerless and stifled? What's one area where you would like more freedom, and how can I best support that?" (AUTONOMY)

- "What parts of your work are you most passionate about? Where do you experience the most disinterest or demotivation? How much of your time is spent in passionate work versus disinterested work? How do you feel about that ratio?" (PASSION)

- "What do you find FUN that we currently do in our organization, and what do you find less enjoyable? What are the first five adjectives you would use to describe your work environment personally? With your FUN motive in mind, how do you feel when you look at that list?" (FUN)

Imagine another scenario, where your team gets together to talk about motives, to hear everyone's perspective, solve problems that need solving, and share motive stories.

Your boss asks you and your team . . .

- "When have you felt most valued and appreciated on this team by others, and when was a time when you have felt less appreciated? What are meaningful ways someone could show you appreciation?" (PEER APPRECIATION)

- "What has made you feel most proud about working for our company, and when have you felt the least pride? What are a few things you wish our company or team could do to elevate our PRESTIGE either within the organization or to the outside world?" (PRESTIGE)

- "Of all your interests and commitments outside of work, which are your five most important? How do you feel about the amount of time you spend on those? What specific obstacles are standing in the way? What is one change you could personally make to allow more time for these things? What is one change you would make in how our team operates to be more efficient and free up time?" (WORK-LIFE HARMONY)

Engaging in these conversations that are led with curiosity, that are a part of the cultural norms, feels safer, more inviting, and open.

"When it comes to creating psychological safety, there is nothing more powerful than asking good questions."

—Amy Edmundson

Curiosity and "good questions," as Amy Edmundson puts it, are a powerful bridge builder to create greater vulnerability, trust, and psychological safety. Employees may not be 100% honest, maybe only 30% or 70%, but that's better than 0% if you never asked the question. If these discussions go well and employees feel heard and there aren't any negative consequences for sharing, then that 30% may grow to 50%, and that 70% to 80%. Peter Brace, PhD, who is a psychological safety and leadership consultant, says, "Psychological safety is a team quality that emerges by itself when the right conditions are created. Our role is to help to create those conditions."[1] You can't force people to trust you or feel psychologically safe, but you can do your best to create the conditions that promote this.

CREATING COURAGEOUS COMMUNICATORS

"Great teams do not hold back with one another. They are unafraid to air their dirty laundry. They admit their mistakes, their weaknesses, and their concerns without fear of reprisal."

—Patrick Lencioni, *The Five Dysfunctions of a Team: A Leadership Fable*

One study found that 80% of employees are avoiding at least one difficult conversation at work, yet having these types of convos is vital for the health of motives.[2] Your goal is absolutely to get to a place where people feel comfortable being compassionately candid, where they don't second-guess if they should tell you they need more guidance from you as a manager (MANAGER SUPPORT) or that they don't respect the way something is being handled unethically with customers (PRESTIGE). Or to share outwardly with the team if they feel they are being underappreciated (PEER APPRECIATION), or that they can't perform their best because some people aren't pulling their weight (ACHIEVEMENT).

Patrick Lencioni, author of *The Five Dysfunctions of a Team: A Leadership Fable*, cites fear of conflict as one of the five main team dysfunctions.[3] I've seen this firsthand in team workshops—absolute crickets when trying to dive into what's not going so hot with some motives and what can be improved. When this happens, it's particularly helpful to break people into smaller groups to tackle these questions because then their suggestions and feedback are from the "group" and not one person feeling they are setting themselves up to be in the hot seat. If you anticipate you might hear crickets when tackling motive problems, then that's a sign you aren't operating from courageous communication but fearful communication. It takes practice, skill, and coaching to build courageous communicators; you can't expect it to happen on its own.

LET'S TALK ABOUT THE GOOD STUFF TOO

Talking about the "good stuff" matters a lot, and what's going well with motives isn't talked about enough. Silence also quiets the positive conversations. I've witnessed the camaraderie, momentum, positivity, and gratitude when people share motive stories that include what's working well, the appreciation for others' support, or how a motive area used to be weak and now it's strong. **You want to remind employees of the great stuff you already have going on and the effort you and others make on the team.**

Following are a few things I've heard when groups have gotten together to talk about their motives at work.

- At a digital agency, someone shared how his coworker, who was the project manager on his account, supported his BALANCED PACE motive and pushed back on unreasonable deadlines with a client. He said he felt pressure and stress as all the feedback came pouring in, but his coworker reached out to him and said, "I'll handle this with the client. You are doing a great job, and we will figure out how to get them what they need in a reasonable amount of time." He said it meant a lot to him that he felt his coworker had his back with this client who could at times be unfairly demanding.

- Someone in a physical therapy office shared how their FUN motive comes to life by being able to do funny videos for Tik-Tok and social media as part of their marketing efforts. She said she enjoys doing them and it brings out her creative side. Funnily enough, another person said thank you for doing them because that is *not* my thing, my opposite of FUN, and thank you for not forcing me to join in.

- After a workshop, one CEO said to me what she appreciated most was hearing why people loved working there. She of course knew they were a company that cared a lot about culture—they are a consultancy that helps their clients with their own culture initiatives. But it was incredibly uplifting to hear firsthand the stories of how her employees appreciated having AUTONOMY, that they felt their TRUSTWORTHY LEADERSHIP motive was the strongest it's been at any company they worked for, and that they felt INNOVATION was possible because of the quality of work everyone contributed. She said she realized they didn't sing their own praises enough and that they should. She wanted to share with new potential hires that her company cares about these needs and is incredibly strong in them. And they are always proactively working to strengthen any motives that are weaker.

CARLOS'S STORY

A motive story that always sticks with me was from Carlos. I mentioned him in chapter 5. Carlos is a sales account manager at a financial tech company. His motives live in two domains only, Company Connection and Advancement. See image 16.1.

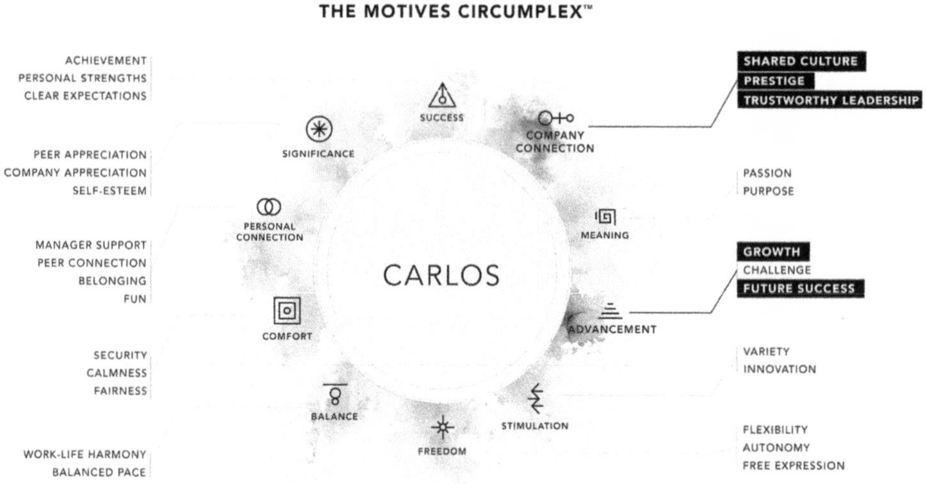

THE MOTIVES CIRCUMPLEX™

Image 16.1

Carlos's well-being meter was looking strong.

- TRUSTWORTHY LEADERSHIP—Thriving

- SHARED CULTURE—Thriving

- PRESTIGE—Thriving

- GROWTH—Coasting

- FUTURE SUCCESS—Coasting

Carlos shared his motive story and why he felt so connected to the company with the desire to grow into the C-suite one day. He says:

I started working here just doing temporary work that I got from a temp agency answering customer service phone calls. For me this job was a big step up. I arrived from Brazil to America when I was nineteen years old. I didn't know English and I barely had any money. I had started doing construction work but was really terrible at it and constantly getting hurt. I was determined to learn English so I could open up more work possibilities and become a US citizen. I learned enough and got a job bagging groceries at a grocery store. I had to walk 2.5 miles in the Boston winter there and back, but it was a step in the right direction, and I continued to study to get better. I then worked my way up into restaurants serving where I could have Post-it notes of the Portuguese words for things as cheat sheets on the ordering system. I worked my way up to management, I perfected my English, and my career started to grow into corporate companies helping with customer service, and eventually I arrived here.

One day I walked up to one of the VP's offices who was nice and always said hi to me, and I knocked on his door. I asked him if I was allowed to sell things. He was very confused by my question. I told him that people were calling with issues and it seemed like there was an opportunity for me to sell some other products we had, and could I try? On the spot he asked me if I wanted a full-time sales job. I didn't have the "right" resume or even a college degree, but he took a chance on me. This company took a chance on me and has treated me well ever since.

I continue to be able to push myself and grow here, and I feel a lot of pride when I can share this story with others, that I work somewhere that gave me this opportunity.

Carlos has worked there now for twelve years. A few of his coworkers in the room that day had heard part of this story, but none of them had heard it like this, even his boss. Everyone left the room that day knowing Carlos for more of his human self and feeling proud to work for the company they worked for. Talk about the good stuff. If there isn't any good stuff to talk about, then you have some work to do.

Discussions related to motives don't always happen naturally in the day-to-day flow of work, especially with the shift to more people working remotely. There aren't the same opportunities for lunch, grabbing a coffee together, waiting together before a meeting, or casually strolling into someone's office to chat. That's why you need to make an intentional effort to make these conversations happen, to get people in the same room (or at least the same Zoom room) and ask questions.

Curiosity also inspires knowing and learning. Yes, asking questions makes probing into areas of weakness or improvement easier, but it also sparks conversation that leads to knowing people for the humans that they are and also for learning interesting and beneficial things about them. Going to you as my boss to share where I want my career to be in the next five years for my FUTURE SUCCESS motive is not a "tough conversation" per se, but it simply might be a conversation that never happens in the routine of the day. It could get buried by busyness, or because of limiting beliefs, thinking that I'm being needy or bothering you.

TALK TO THE PEOPLE YOU LEAD, AND SET THE STAGE

The motives assessment opens the door and initiates motive conversations, but once you get these conversations going, you want to keep them going for the long haul. You want there to be more "formal" and "informal" communication regarding needs in your workplace. You should have formal set communication, including regularly scheduled one-on-one meetings with employees or "stay interviews" and meetings with teams, managers, or appropriate groups to engage in motive stories. Weaving motive conversations into town hall gatherings, round table discussions, lunch and learns, team off-sites, and monthly meetings is easy. "Entry interviews" are also important as part of onboarding. What better way to welcome a new employee, get to know them, and make them believe their health and happiness matters than learning their motives, understanding from the get-go how to meet them, and hearing their motive story?

Talking to the people you lead will take time and energy. It will take courageous communication and maybe won't feel super comfortable for you, especially at first. But that will change over time if you start doing it. Some leaders I've worked with love this part of the pathway, and others want to somehow wave a magic wand where a quicker way or a solution that doesn't involve them talking and listening appears. I was talking with a culture manager at an IT company who wanted help with well-being and psychological safety. She said these were two of the five main pillars for her to focus on that year in her role. I shared some background with her, the assessment, and our software platform we created that helps facilitate these meaningful conversations around motives. She came back to me and said, "My managers don't have time to do this. They want something easier. Is there a shortcut you can give me?" I told her there are no shortcuts. If you want to be a "people first" leader, then you need to talk to employees.

I want to talk more about these one-on-one and group conversations, but whether you are going to be talking with one person or twenty, setting the stage is important. The purpose of the conversation is about *them*—to connect with them on a deeper level, to hear their honest thoughts and truths. Invite them to share what they feel comfortable sharing.

ONE-ON-ONE MOTIVE CONVERSATIONS

You have heard me say many times throughout these pages that to be a leader people want to work for, and be in a position to help your employees thrive, you must know your people. To do that you must speak with them, one-on-one, about their needs. Remember when I shared my story of taking my team members off-site to try to figure out what they needed and wanted at work? Those conversations were a game-changer for both them and me, but they would have been so much more effective if I had known their motives and had asked good questions related to their specific motives. Sure, asking, "What do you need to be happy?" or "What's going well or not well for you?" is a start, and it's better than nothing. But when you know someone needs FLEXIBILITY to have PURPOSE or SECURITY, you will get much deeper insight by talking about those needs specifically and asking powerful questions like those I shared above. You can ask questions related to motive stories, how strong or weak your team members feel their motives are, but knowing your employees' specific needs will help you to ask questions related to those needs.

The ability to know each person you lead on a deeper individual level is going to be more challenging the more people you lead; knowing ten people well is easier than knowing two hundred. But let me give you a little inspiration: Monty Moran, who was the CEO of Chipotle and was responsible for creating an incredible culture and driving enormous business results to build a Fortune 500 company, met with over twenty thousand employees and had one-on-one conversations with each one. Twenty thousand employees. Let that sink in. In his book *Love Is Free. Guac Is Extra.: How Vulnerability, Empowerment, and Curiosity Built an Unstoppable Team*, he shares, "During my time with Chipotle, I had over 20,000 one-on-ones with crew members in our restaurants, and hundreds in the corporate office as well. People often asked where I found the time to talk to them, get to know them, and understand them, with such a big company to run. But the reality was, I had such a big company to run that I could not afford not to sit down and talk to them. Caring for, understanding, and knowing our people gave me a reputation for caring deeply. And while I could never meet with all 70,000 of our employees, this reputation spread, and engendered incredible loyalty on the part of our people, and led them to devote their full energy to their work."[4]

If the CEO of a Fortune 500 company can do it, *you* can do it. If you are a senior leader, you should also empower your managers to do it. Also realize that the time spent to be proactive and preventive up front, to care about your people now instead of when they are about to leave, to discover small issues now instead of when they have become a huge problem, is smart. It's taking a purposeful, mindful approach. Beyond that, you are setting an example that will rub off on others. If you sit down with a manager who reports to you to talk about their motives, to show you give a damn, to understand what they need and why, and see what support they might need, that manager is more likely to turn around and have that conversation with their team. It creates a ripple effect, especially if you give them tools to help them do it. And let me tell you, they need the tools! At the end of these conversations you should have a few goals and action items, which we'll talk about on the next and final step of the pathway.

GROUP MOTIVE CONVERSATIONS

Doing a motive workshop is a great way to get talking about motives within your team, among your managers, or elsewhere in your company. How you decide to structure your workshop, meeting, coaching session (whatever you want to call it!) will depend on factors such as length of time, size of the group, in-person versus virtual, degree of psychological safety, and your personal objectives. There are so many different motive exercises you can do, but I will walk you through some great options to inspire you.

SHARE MOTIVE STORIES

Have people share their top 5 motives and some of their motive stories. You can select prompts from the motive stories worksheet we shared in chapter 9 that you think would be most valuable for your group, and ask attendees to think about their prompts and share. Suggested prompts: Why are these needs important to them? What motive is the most meaningful right now and why? What is something the team may not know about you as it relates to a motive? If you have a larger group, you can have people break into smaller groups and share that way.

MEETING MOTIVES TOGETHER

The purpose of this exercise is to come together to share thoughts, experiences, and ideas to change, elevate, and celebrate the 28 needs for your team or organization. It's an opportunity to work through strengthening the collective motives of the group and also motives in your culture. It's not on you alone to honor, protect, and strengthen motives. You need to get everyone involved and gather ideas from people with different perspectives. Employees will give you great insight and ideas if you give them the chance to develop and share them.

Select a few motives that you want the group to focus on while also offering the opportunity to ideate on motive areas of interest. For example, for the case study group we have been talking about throughout the book, we determined we wanted to make sure people focused on the top motives of the group, the nine motives listed, and to make sure to have ample discussion on the motives in the drowning/surviving bucket from the *EVALUATE* step, the weaker met motives.

MOTIVES HEALTH SCORECARD		MOTIVE HEALTH
MOTIVES *Most important motives for the group*		**MOTIVE HEALTH** *Drowning, suffering, coasting, thriving*
MOTIVE 1:	WORK/LIFE HARMONY	Drowning
MOTIVE 2:	PEER CONNECTION	Suffering
MOTIVE 3:	GROWTH	Suffering
MOTIVE 4:	TRUSTWORTHY LEADERSHIP	Suffering
MOTIVE 5:	CALMNESS	Coasting
MOTIVE 6:	INNOVATION	Coasting
MOTIVE 7:	FUTURE SUCCESS	Coasting
MOTIVE 8:	FLEXIBILITY	Thriving
MOTIVE 9:	PASSION	Thriving

Image 16.2

Next, you break the group into smaller subgroups and have them ideate together and designate one group leader per group who will share the group's ideas with the larger group. Provide a few questions to guide discussion.

- As a team or company, why do we do well with *<this motive>* or why do we struggle with it?

- Give a specific example of when you felt *<this motive>* was met or when it was not met for you or others.

- Why do I find *<this motive>* challenging or feel it's strong?

- What is an idea, belief, behavior, or way *<this motive>* could be supported and enhanced, whether small or big?

- Where do we already do well with *<this motive>* that we want to maintain or elevate even further?

Bring the larger group back together, and have the leader of each subgroup share their ideas and talk about them collectively. Make sure you have someone capturing the ideas throughout the meeting. At the end of the meeting identify takeaways, top ideas, and next steps; let people know you will follow up with more details. These ideas will be used to help you develop your final People-First Action Plan to meet motives.

PUTTING INSIGHTS INTO ACTION
HAVE ONE-ON-ONE MOTIVE CONVERSATIONS WITH YOUR EMPLOYEES

Once employees have their top motives, get your one-on-one meetings with them on the calendar. Lead with curiosity, and decide a few motive questions you want to ask each person ahead of time based on their unique motives. You should send those questions to each person before you meet with them, as this gives them time to think about the questions and prepare a bit so they aren't thrown off guard.

HAVE GROUP/TEAM MOTIVE CONVERSATIONS

Get people together to have motive conversations. Being able to do this in person is always great. If you have an off-site coming up or company event you can work it into, then fantastic! If not, you can absolutely do this virtually. What we would recommend is that you choose one or the other. Having half the people there in person and half virtual doesn't usually work the best.

MODEL, INITIATE, AND REWARD THE COURAGEOUS COMMUNICATION YOU WANT TO SEE

What you want to see in others is what you must hold yourself accountable to. If you want people to show up bravely, candidly, and not run away from constructive conflict, then you need to demonstrate these yourself, signaling what you want others to do in return. Share your motive story, display vulnerability, and prompt people to share what they need from others. Reward and thank people when they share. Don't bury tension; make it normal that issues with unresolved tension get talked about in the right way. Coach your employees on how to be courageous communicators or seek out outside coaching and resources to help.

DO A SELF-CHECK-IN

Being more curious about who the people are both in and outside of work and the needs that drive them will benefit you and them. To what degree do you feel you lead with curiosity? Do you informally talk about needs at work and ask people questions related to motives? Is this something you can do more of?

CHAPTER 17

COMMITTING TO PUTTING PEOPLE FIRST

We have arrived at the final step on the Motives Met Pathway for you as a leader, to *MEET MOTIVES*. Now is the fun part. Take all the insights you have uncovered and actions you have already taken to solidify your People-First Action Plan to meet motives.

First things first. As a person and a leader, you have cared enough about the health and happiness of your employees at work to read this book and get this far. That itself is worth something. Your intentions are good. Intentions do matter, because meeting these human needs at work isn't going to be flawless. But if your people know you care, know you want them to thrive and that you are trying, that *does* matter and will take you far. But without commitment to action, intentions don't matter enough.

From the first pages I have shown you why motives matter for your employees, for you, and for your business. But that doesn't mean that Dream Killer #10 might not stand in your way—that health and happiness at work won't be the priority it needs to be. Even if you have arrived at the almost final chapter in this book, it still doesn't mean you are fully a "believer." Part of you might still be a bit of a "disbeliever" and not fully committed. Some part of you might still be thinking this isn't your responsibility or you don't want it to be your responsibility. You may be a manager or someone who leads other managers who just wants to manage the work and not lead your employees. Maybe you don't like the "people stuff." Or maybe you aren't naturally good at the "people stuff" and haven't been given the help to get better at it. Whether you like it or not, are good at it or not, or believe it's your responsibility or not, you do in fact have the responsibility. Research shows that managers have more impact on a person's mental health than their therapist and doctors, and equal impact to their spouse or partner.[1] The degree to which people's motives will not only be healthy but have the ability to flourish will significantly be impacted by you. So it's time to rise to the occasion.

Even for those believers who have stepped into full ownership and responsibility, commitment can waver, and I will own this myself because I can struggle too. Yes, my employees' mental health is important, but I have all this other stuff to do, so once I have the time then I'll focus on my motives. Yes, my employees' happiness is important, but my primary job is to deliver results. Yes, meeting motives is important, but my own boss doesn't seem to care, so I guess I can't care.

Yes, well-being is important, but . . . There can be a lot of "buts." The reality is things like hitting deadlines, increasing revenue numbers, hiring new people, improving customer service, and putting out fires ends up coming first. **Consciously you are committed to prioritizing your people, but these other unconscious commitments**

win out. When you do put people over profits, when you truly put people first, they deliver. They make the profits happen, hit the deadlines, deliver results, extinguish fires quicker, and stay at your company longer. There is a fundamental difference between being truly committed to something and just interested in something. Interest gives you an out to only do it when you want to, when it's convenient or easy. When you fully commit, your only option is to follow through on your commitment.

It can be easy for all of these other things to come first and divert your attention, and it's also easy to stick with the same way of doing things or revert back to the old way of doing things. Change and growth is worth it, and it may be something you deeply desire. You might even believe it's of top importance, but it won't always be easy. It can be hard, and when things get hard, sometimes we want to quit.

So before we jump into the exciting work of solidifying your People-First Action Plan, we need to make sure that you are committed to making well-being essential, for you personally as a leader *and* for your employees. It's not a nice-to-have; it's a must-have. It's not a one-and-done thing; the Motives Met Pathway is a new way of working and leading. As the saying goes, the road to hell is paved with good intentions. Intentions alone are not enough; they need to guide you into committed action. This is your new beginning.

DEEPENING YOUR COMMITMENT

"How you spend your days is a direct, honest reflection of your truest priorities. There is no exception."   **—Susie Moore**

Implementing the desired actions in your action plan will require resources—your time and attention, some energy and dollars. Without these things, you aren't really committing. You need to make the time to tend to these needs personally: the time to have the one-on-ones we just talked about on the *COMMUNICATE* step. The time to get your team together to talk about motives. The time to do the personal actions you are going to do to support motives for your people. For most leaders and managers, priorities make it to their calendars; they block and schedule time. You need to do the same here and protect the time you need to devote attention and energy to support motives in your workplace.

You also need to give your employees time: time to be purposeful and reflect on their needs, give their needs the attention they deserve, and to do the things they need to do to meet their needs. Time to be purposeful with others' motives, to give support, to build a culture of compassion and care. If your employees have their day jam-packed from the moment they start work to the moment they end it day in and day out, then don't expect their motives to be met. Sadly, this is how so many organizations operate. Employees' days are stuffed to the brim, and that may be your reality too. Employees in this situation have no time to even think about how to meet their motives, let alone take action.

If I have the GROWTH motive and I want to attend those webinars, read those books, take that course, or find mentors, these things won't happen. If I have the INNOVATION motive, the time to try new things won't happen because I will be scrambling just to finish the constant deadlines. FUN? Yeah, there isn't going to be a whole lot of that happening either. If someone asks for help, I most likely won't have the bandwidth to give it, let alone go out of my way to be thinking about simple things I could do that week to proactively support someone or do something nice to complement a motive.

Last, dollars. There are many ways to support motives that cost nothing. There are many ways to support motives that cost a tiny bit or a lot, but budgets are necessary. You might want to hold a few off-sites in person every year to get people together who work remotely to connect. You might need to hire outside experts to help make big changes around your DEI efforts. You might want to invest in new innovative software systems. Maybe you need funds for leadership training or fun events. If you aren't financially supporting your employees' health and happiness at work, then you aren't truly supporting it. You need to put your money where your mouth is.

Before you roll up your sleeves to map out your People-First Action Plan, I'll briefly revisit the main areas you want to consider, now from the leader and organizational vantage point. Remember that meeting motives requires both thought and action.

THOUGHT

Mindset, beliefs, and attitudes are a significant part of meeting motives. Have you created the shared meaning for people to think about well-being at work in the same way? Where as a team or a company do we hold unconscious commitments and beliefs that block motives? Where do we need to create mindset shifts to strengthen motives? Do we say we value CALMNESS, but we believe we need to say yes to every client deadline request, even when they are unreasonable? Do we need to adopt the mindset that if we aren't failing we aren't innovating enough to support INNOVATION?

ACTION

What are concrete actions we can take to support motives? If we value FAIRNESS, have we considered our degree of pay transparency? If we value TRUSTWORTHY LEADERSHIP, do we actively seek out ways to get feedback from employees on how leaders are doing? Additionally, where are we taking action but can do better? Rather than just use rainbow marketing during Pride Month to reinforce BELONGING, could we support an LGBTQ+ nonprofit and help raise funds and awareness?

Remember the to-don'ts can be just as important as the to-dos. It's putting a stake in the ground and saying we are no longer going to waste time on tasks that don't move the needle of the business significantly to reach our desired FUTURE SUCCESS. We are no longer going to hire for "culture fit," bringing in the same perspectives by hiring the same types of people. It will be for "culture add," people who align with values but bring diverse experiences, perspectives, and ideas to enhance our SHARED CULTURE. We will no longer be constantly sending off-hours/weekend emails or chat messages to reinforce our commitment to WORK-LIFE HARMONY.

MEETING MOTIVES MEANS CONTROLLING THE CONTROLLABLES

Your job is to use your influence where possible and to control what you can control. You can't force someone on the team to be kind, but you can address hostile behavior hurting PEER CONNECTION immediately by making it clear that this behavior is not welcome here. You can't force other leaders to give COMPANY

APPRECIATION, but you can inspire when you show meaningful appreciation to employees. You can't force people to have FUN, but you provide the means for them to create FUN.

MEETING MOTIVES IS ABOUT TAKING BIG OR DIFFICULT STEPS

Whether it's hiring new roles to better manage workload, implementing longer parental leave, turning away business from problematic clients or customers, or letting go of leaders who are untrustworthy, at times tougher choices and/or bigger actions are how you create an organization where motives are strong and protected. It may mean walking away from the way "things have always been done" and being open-minded to experimenting and trying new things to see if they work. Maybe you need to reassess overhauling your operations and current systems to optimize for efficiency and a better BALANCED PACE for employees. It could be developing a new mission with more meaning that creates greater PURPOSE. It might be completely changing roles and responsibilities on a team to better align with PERSONAL STRENGTHS.

MEETING MOTIVES IS ABOUT TAKING THE LITTLE OR SIMPLE STEPS

On the other side, meeting motives can be about the impactful yet smaller actions and habits such as changing a norm; the leader in the room might speak last in order to encourage everyone to speak up and share their opinions (FREE EXPRESSION). Or everyone might express gratitude to one person who has helped them in the group in your monthly meetings (PEER APPRECIATION).

MEETING MOTIVES IS ABOUT RECEIVING HELP FROM OTHERS

Whether they're internal or external people, who are your "whos"? Are there people you need to get approval or support from to implement ideas for your team or get the budget you need?

Are there other leaders who would be interested in getting together to develop a People-First Action Plan, someone who's also passionate about health and happiness at work? If you get employees together who are advocates, they will come up with some great ideas to strengthen motives. For example, Deloitte created the Well-Being Wizards, a network of empowered employees who come together to develop ideas for elevating human well-being within the company.

MEETING MOTIVES MEANS INVESTIGATING AND EXPLORING

You may know you have a problem area you want to work on, that people don't feel you are living your values (SHARED CULTURE), that advancement in your organization feels limited (FUTURE SUCCESS), that insecurity lingers after some people were let go (SECURITY), or that overwhelm is high (CALMNESS). But you might not know how to go about fixing these things . . . yet. Your next step might be to do some research, read a book, reach out to experts, find a coach, check out an online course, or gather ideas from others. Taking the time to explore options and do some "homework" may be an important next step.

MEETING MOTIVES IS ABOUT CELEBRATING AND BEING GRATEFUL

As a leader, looking toward the future is important, determining what you want to fix, change, and grow, but noticing all the ways in which people are thriving and what's working gets overlooked or can feel indulgent. Celebrating success helps people feel included, bonded, motivated, and appreciated. It's important for you to feel good about what's going well, and also for your people to feel it too. This can help lift up motives like FUN, COMPANY APPRECI-ATION, and PRESTIGE, feeling proud to work in a place where motives are strong. In what ways do you celebrate and communicate wins and areas of strength to your employees?

MEETING MOTIVES IS ABOUT PRIORITIZING, ACCEPTING, AND COMPROMISING

You may have many ideas and hopes but only so many resources and opportunities to see those ideas through. You may have motive ideas that hold friction with one another, as we know they will. Prioritizing what makes it into your final action plan today and what doesn't is a tough and critical part of the process. You may also have limitations when it comes to some of these motives more than others, roadblocks that need to be worked through. There could also be a reality that, given the nature of your business or industry, you aren't able to meet certain motives as strongly. You need to accept certain realities and be honest with employees about that reality rather than promising things you can't deliver on.

Now that you are grounded in the areas you want to consider for your action plan, let's put pen to paper and create it in the final *MEET MOTIVES* chapter.

CHAPTER 18

CREATING YOUR PEOPLE-FIRST ACTION PLAN

When developing your action plan, there are three levels to consider: the individual employee, the team/group, and the organizational level. You need to determine how to support the top motives of the employees you lead; how to care for collective motives at the group level; and what broader systems, policies, and cultural factors you want to consider or change to better meet motives at a broader cultural level.

INDIVIDUAL ACTION PLANS

At this point you know the top needs of each of your employees, you know how healthy they are, and have learned all sorts of helpful information related to them from your conversations. Now you want to take all those insights and actually do something with them! When you have the one-on-one conversation with each person, you want to end that meeting with an action plan specifically for that person. You are essentially guiding them to create their personal Work Life Well-Lived Action Plan that we discussed in the Meet Motives chapters, 11 and 12. This is the time for you to step up and be an advocate, coach, and mentor for your employees, to identify problems you can help solve and advice or perspective to support. In hearing people's motive stories and talking through the motive questions you ask, you can help think of different ways to honor, protect, and strengthen motives all while getting to know them better as human beings and creating a closer connection.

Having an action plan for each person isn't complicated. You want to leave the meeting with a few things:

1. Reinforce what's going well: Give the positive things the attention they deserve. Identify what progress has been made and what is already going well. Take notice of interesting or helpful information you learned about that person, and let them know the value you received in having this conversation with them.

2. Identify actions the employee is going to take: How is that person going to elevate their mindset? What are they going to do (or not do!) to meet their motives?

3. Identify actions you/others are going to take: What you are going to do to help support their motives? What are next steps or any follow-ups? Are there things you want the team to discuss? Is there an idea you want to bring to your boss?

The next time you meet with this employee, you will be able to come back to what you discussed. It's also helpful for you to keep a few notes for yourself. How did the discussion go overall? What do you want to keep in mind or remember about this person?

TEAM OR GROUP ACTION PLANS

Now you want to develop a plan to elevate the well-being of the collective community you lead that works together toward common goals. If you have a smaller organization, you can also do this for your organization at large. For bigger organizations, you will want your teams or departments to develop their action plans and then consider broader strategies and actions at the organizational level, which I'll talk about next.

At this point, you—again—have a whole lot of information, insights, and data to strategize from. You have the assessment, you have your well-being analytics, and you have listened to employees in different ways to hear firsthand about these needs and ideas to meet them. If you want to gather more ideas from others, you can do that now or, as you share your thoughts with others, gain more input then. Especially if you did some form of a workshop with your team or group and followed the structure we provided you, you would have left that session with great ideas and even had specific action items already in motion.

It's also an awesome idea to get a group together who is passionate about helping to elevate your workplace; allow them to ideate and bring ideas to you as well. Now is where you add any other ideas you want to consider and then start to narrow your action plan and prioritize. This process is more of an art than a science, and it's going to depend on everything you personally are working with. But the following steps will help guide you.

STEP 1: GATHER YOUR "MEET MOTIVES" IDEAS

SECTION 1:

Start by identifying the top motives of your group, which is something you may have already done. In your team/group circumplex, which motives were of top importance? Maybe there were eight clear top motives you want to start with. Or five first-tier importance and five second-tier importance. Also include the health bucket you assigned each motive to. These are the top motives from our case study group we have been discussing throughout the book.

MOTIVES HEALTH SCORECARD	
MOTIVES Most important motives for the group	**MOTIVE HEALTH** Drowning, suffering, coasting, thriving
MOTIVE 1: WORK/LIFE HARMONY	Drowning
MOTIVE 2: PEER CONNECTION	Suffering
MOTIVE 3: GROWTH	Suffering
MOTIVE 4: TRUSTWORTHY LEADERSHIP	Suffering
MOTIVE 5: CALMNESS	Coasting
MOTIVE 6: INNOVATION	Coasting
MOTIVE 7: FUTURE SUCCESS	Coasting
MOTIVE 8: FLEXIBILITY	Thriving
MOTIVE 9: PASSION	Thriving

Image 18.1

SECTION 2:

Take these motives and decide which motive action area you would place them in—as a change, maintenance, or elevate motive. Think about the motive health ratings as well as your conversations with your employees.

- **Change Motive:** motives that aren't as healthy, where you want results that are different from where they are now.

- **Maintenance Motive:** motives that are doing well that you want to simply stay well.

- **Elevate Motive:** motives that are already healthy, but you have the desire or opportunity to elevate even higher.

MOTIVES ACTION AREA			
MOTIVES		**MOTIVE HEALTH:**	**ACTION AREA:**
MOTIVE 1:	WORK/LIFE HARMONY	Drowning	Change
MOTIVE 2:	PEER CONNECTION	Surviving	Change
MOTIVE 3:	GROWTH	Surviving	Change
MOTIVE 4:	TRUSTWORTHY LEADERSHIP	Surviving	Change
MOTIVE 5:	CALMNESS	Coasting	Elevate
MOTIVE 6:	INNOVATION	Coasting	Change
MOTIVE 7:	FUTURE SUCCESS	Coasting	Elevate
MOTIVE 8:	FLEXIBILITY	Thriving	Maintain
MOTIVE 9:	PASSION	Thriving	Elevate

Image 18.2

SECTION 3:

For each motive from above that you classified as a CHANGE or ELEVATE motive, fill out this section and list potential ideas to honor, protect, and strengthen each motive. Include the ideas you already have from others, and think about any other new ideas you have. It's good to allow yourself to brainstorm, to throw out ideas no matter how realistic or aspirational. For example, if you had the support and resources you needed, what might you try or do? When you narrow down this list, that is when you will wrestle with what is possible or what perhaps is worth pursuing to see if it can be possible.

POTENTIAL MOTIVE ACTIONS

MOTIVE: **WORK-LIFE HARMONY**

How can this motive be protected, honored, and strengthened?

MINDSET

Beliefs, thoughts, attitudes

TO-DOS - SMALL

Little to-dos, micro actions, habits

TO-DOS - BIG

Large to-dos, longer-term goals, ambitious ideas

TO-DON'TS

Boundaries, your "nos," what you will no longer do

SUPPORT

Help from others, your "whos"

Image 18.3

SECTION 4:

MAINTENANCE MOTIVE

If this motive is a MAINTENANCE motive, fill out this section

What do we need to do to "maintain" the health of this motive? _____

Is there anything that threatens keeping this motive healthy? _____

When should we check back in? _____

Image 18.4

SECTION 5:

What other thoughts, ideas, and actions are there around other motives that haven't been covered yet that you want to consider? In your team meeting or conversation with others, there may be ideas related to motives that weren't in the top most important motives for the team, for example, but you absolutely may want to still take actions or explore options. Maybe FUN wasn't a top motive for the group but there were some great ideas around something new and FUN for the company outing this year. Maybe PURPOSE wasn't a top motive but there was great discussion around what people find meaningful at work and ideas to amplify that meaning.

ADDITIONAL MOTIVE ACTIONS

Ideas for other motives that didn't rise to the top

MOTIVE: **FUN**

Ideas:

_____

_____

_____

MOTIVE: **FAIRNESS**

Ideas:

_____

_____

_____

Image 18.5

STEP 2: PRIORITIZE AND FINALIZE YOUR ACTION PLAN

This is the tough part. You may not be able to do everything at once, so you need to narrow down priorities, delegate, and weigh options. It's also good to have other people give their thoughts here, and you may again already have some priorities coming out of your team workshop or meeting. These are the things you want to consider that are similar to your individual action plan:

- Impact—What impact will this have on honoring, protecting, and strengthening this motive? Low, medium, high?

- Difficulty level—Is this easy, medium, or hard?

- Resources—What time, energy, money, or support do I have? What time, energy, money, or support do I need? If what I have and what I need aren't in alignment, can I get them in alignment?

- Importance and urgency—Which actions are important and urgent? Which ones seem urgent but are just distractions? Which ones could be delayed?

- Desire—Which ideas/actions seem of the highest interest to me and my team or organization?

One filter that I always use with clients in the decision-making process is to like your "why." As you are determining what stays and what goes, ask yourself the why behind your choice. Does it make sense? Will others feel it makes sense? Is there a good reason to keep or cut? For example, if employees want to be able to wear jeans in the office on no-client-meeting days and they are told no because that's the way it's always been, that isn't going to feel good to them. And yes, this is a real-life example (insert eye-roll emoji here).

You might also need buy-in from others at this point in the process. Is there an idea you want to bring to senior leadership to see if they will get on board? Do you need to secure the budget with someone? Do you want to get a gut-check of how some people on your team who might be apprehensive will feel if you follow through with an idea? Now is the time to get the green light or red light from your "whos" so you can make informed decisions for your action plan. Some of you might be dealing with constant red lights, people who are "disbelievers" and make meeting motives a tough pursuit.

You can only control your controllables. But this book, this process and research give you some ammo. When you bring to the table research, proof, data, and feedback from your employees, it makes it tougher for others to argue with.

STEP 3: COMMIT

Help deepen your commitment by answering these last few questions.

Commitment questions:

- What benefits will we get if we follow through on these motive action-plan items?
- What can I anticipate might be difficult?
- How will we keep going when things get hard?
- What will it cost us if I don't follow through?

STEP 4: DELEGATE AND DETERMINE ROI

Once you have narrowed down the final elements of your People-First Action Plan, assign responsibilities and delegate where necessary. This is also where you can now determine where you want to be.

What would make this a win? Positive employee feedback? Seeing your motive health metrics improve to a desired degree? More promotions within the company for GROWTH? Testing a certain amount of ideas for INNOVATION? What would make you feel the return on investment was positive?

STEP 5: SHARE YOUR PLAN

Now you get to communicate to your employees that you are taking action to take well-being seriously. Share your action plan; get employees excited about it and involved. It's also important to share why you have chosen the action that you have. When employees understand the "why" behind your decisions, they are more likely to get on board, *if* the why is compelling.

ORGANIZATIONAL ACTION PLANS

This third level is taking a broader approach, considering policies, structures, and cultural norms. Some of this thinking can come to life in your team or group action plans as well, but this is where you want to take a step back at a higher level and assess all 28 motives, to ask yourself, and perhaps other leaders as well: As an organization, where do we do well and not so well? This is particularly important for senior leaders, generally people who affect larger-scale initiatives and decisions. You may also have ideas come up on your team that would be a higher-level decision that you might have to get buy-in from your boss or others.

In earlier chapters we talked about doing a personal motive audit to reflect on your personal motive influence. Now you want to do a company motive audit. What actions do we want to take at a company-wide level? As managers or other leaders meet with their teams, they may come up with ideas that would impact not just their team, but the broader organization as a whole. They may need approval to implement these things and ask you to consider them. If a team comes up with a great idea for a motive area, that team leader could share that with other leaders and exchange ideas.

Once your managers and other leaders have gone through the Motives Met Pathway, you can then get everyone together to work through an organization action plan.

Have leaders (including yourself) think about the following:

- Where are we strong and where are we weak with the 28 motives? In the last year, what are specific examples of when we have done well and not so well? What needs to change? Are there trends across the organization of thriving and drowning motives?

- What ideas did your specific teams come up with? What parts of your action plan might we want or need to consider at a broader level across the organization? What are your recommendations to consider? Where do you need approval?

- How do we become an organization that is meeting our people's needs, which in turn will also make us more successful? What are other companies doing that we might want to try? What are best practices or forward-thinking ideas we should consider? You have to remember, what works for one company might not work for yours, but you want to explore, keep an open-mind, and be willing to experiment.

It can also be helpful to think about good questions as it relates to each motive to stimulate great ideas.

- What is our tolerance for risk? How do we handle failure? (INNOVATION)

- Do we honor diverse cultures with floating rather than fixed holidays where employees are able to take time off based on personal needs, or cultural and religious backgrounds? (BELONGING)

- To what degree do people feel familiar with our leadership, who we are as people, what we care about and our vision for the company? (TRUSTWORTHY LEADERSHIP)

- Do we have supportive parental leave policies or family leave for those caring for ill or elderly family members? (FLEXIBILITY).

- Are we hindering employees from taking enough personal time off by offering unlimited PTO instead of generous PTO, which has led to employees taking less time off because of fear of overstepping and that they don't want to be viewed as slackers? (WORK-LIFE HARMONY)

- Do we have clear values at our company that we live by and align with our employees' values? (SHARED CULTURE)

- Are we inhibiting advancement by promoting people to management positions from within, or are we always recruiting from outside the organization first without giving our loyal employees an opportunity? (GROWTH)

- Have we coached our people on how to build trust and psychological safety? (FREE EXPRESSION)

- Do we show employees we appreciate not just what they do but who they are as people? (COMPANY APPRECIATION)

Give people these questions ahead of time so they can have a bit of incubation time and some good thoughts prepared. When you get everyone together to talk through these things, you will have some amazing ideas to work with. The next step is to create a version of the plan that goes through the same steps for the team/group level we just went through.

I want to end this leadership part of the book by reassuring you that developing and implementing your People-First Action Plan is not something that happens overnight. It takes time to walk the pathway, and it's a continuous walk that never ends. This is your opportunity to simply start, take it a step at a time, enjoy the process, and allow it to grow and become a part of your culture.

I want to leave you with some words of inspiration of the types of leaders we can decide to be from an admirable advocate of a more human work world. Jen Fisher is a human sustainability leader at Deloitte. She was their first chief well-being officer. She is also the author of *Work Better Together: How to Cultivate Strong Relationships to Maximize Well-Being and Boost Bottom Lines* and editor at large for Thrive Global. In her impactful TEDx Talk, "The Future of Work," she says these words:

> The skill set for what makes a great leader is changing, and while operational, financial, and technical skills will always be relevant, what's needed now is human skills. And here's what I think this leader looks like. They don't just focus on the bottom

line because they know without good people there is no bottom line. They don't just reward you for how you grow sales, they reward you for how you help grow people. They don't just believe that high productivity is a measure for good well-being because they know it can also be a signal for burnout. They don't just invest in the latest employee wellness programs, they invest in creating company cultures that are committed to human sustainability. And they don't just define our value in life by the work that we do because they know that work is just one of many inputs to a well-lived life.[1]

Now I want to know the ONE next step you are going to take after you finish reading this book. No matter how small it is, determine where you will go from here.

People-First Workplace

My next step to leading a people-first workplace is . . .

Image 18.6

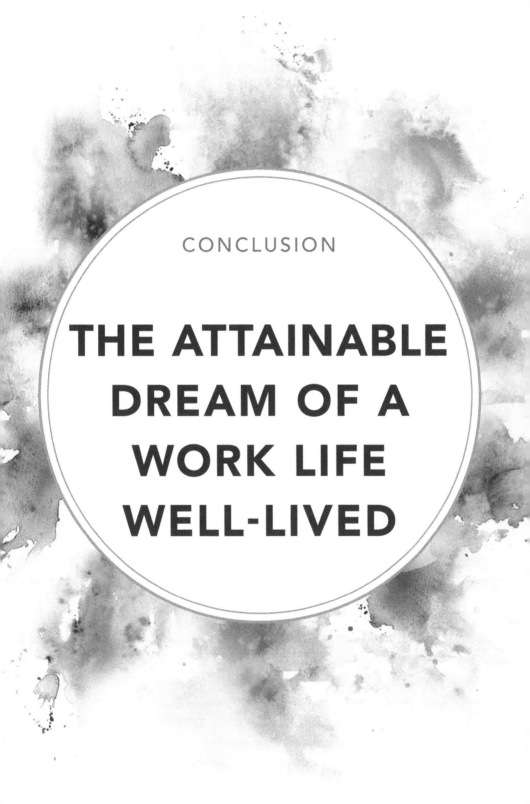

CONCLUSION

THE ATTAINABLE DREAM OF A WORK LIFE WELL-LIVED

CHAPTER 19

LIVING THE WORK LIFE WELL-LIVED PRINCIPLES

Regardless of job title, industry, or degree of work happiness and wellness, a thread that runs through the people who embraced the Motives Met No-B.S. way forward is the feeling of empowerment they have shared with me. Empowerment means you're becoming stronger and more confident, better able to control your life and claim what's rightfully yours. You become empowered to elevate your health and happiness at work, to have the well-being you deserve, and to support and lead others in their work well-being journey to have that too.

SIMPLE BUT NOT EASY

"Life is really simple, but we insist on making it complicated."

—Confucius

When it comes down to it, it's not complicated. Motives Met illuminates the most often overlooked simplicity of being well at work. It's common sense that to have well-being we have to meet our human needs, starting with the ones that matter most. Those top needs will differ by person, those needs will shift over time, and when they are cared for, good things will happen for ourselves, our relationships, and our organizations. Simple, however, doesn't always mean easy, and there are ten dream killers that stand in our way.

- Dream Killer #1: We don't really know what work well-being is.

- Dream Killer #2: We think we know "the answer" to what creates our best work lives and workplaces, but it's often not the "best" answer.

- Dream Killer #3: We push short-term Band-Aid solutions, but they don't work.

- Dream Killer #4: We don't know who to trust because of too many conflicting opinions and an overwhelming amount of information.

- Dream Killer #5: We don't bring our humanity to work.

- Dream Killer #6: We take a passive or reactive approach to caring for health and happiness at work, not a preventive and proactive one.

- Dream Killer #7: We don't show up in meaningful ways to co-create well-being at work together.

- Dream Killer #8: We don't evaluate and measure well-being in the way we should.

- Dream Killer #9: We don't talk about what we need most at work with ourselves and others.

- Dream Killer #10: We don't prioritize health and happiness at work enough.

When you follow the Motives Met Pathway and live your action plan, these dream killers won't get in your way.

DEEPENING YOUR "MOTIVES MINDSET"

Throughout these chapters, you have been cultivating what we call the "Motives Mindset"—the thoughts, attitudes, and beliefs surrounding motives, or needs, to help you create the greatest well-being in your work life, workplace, and work relationships. To help you further develop and deepen the Motives Mindset, we developed our Work Life Well-Lived Principles, aka "laws to live by." The ideas here are not new; they are a summary of the main takeaways from the book that you will want to revisit. If you are a leader, these principles are what you need to embed into your team and organization. These principles are what you need to hold yourself and others accountable to.

THE TEN WORK LIFE WELL-LIVED PRINCIPLES

- **WLWL Principle #1**—All motives matter, but well-being is personal; it's about personal needs and embracing motive diversity.

- **WLWL Principle #2**—The focus must be on the needs that require each person's greatest attention in the present, but they will change.

- **WLWL Principle #3**—People cannot, nor should they have to try to, escape being human beings with human emotions at work.

- **WLWL Principle #4**—Be curious; seek to understand yourself and create your motive story and to understand others and hear theirs.

- **WLWL Principle #5**—People must show up with motive mindfulness in their work life and work relationships on purpose, with purpose.

- **WLWL Principle #6**—Supporting others in their well-being is a win for all.

- **WLWL Principle #7**—Motives must be spoken about honestly, courageously, and with good intentions, to meet motives.

- **WLWL Principle #8**—Motives cannot be elevated if they aren't evaluated.

- **WLWL Principle #9**—Big actions can be necessary, but change does not need to be big to be meaningful; small things can also be significant to meet motives.

- **WLWL Principle #10**—Get comfortable being uncomfortable; sometimes meeting motives is about vulnerability, courage, and resilience.

MAKING OUR DREAM A REALITY

"Hope lies in dreams, in imagination, and in the courage of those who dare to make dreams into reality."   **—Jonas Salk**

I always find my way back to this statistic: On average, one-third of our precious lives is spent working. **A well-lived life means we must have a work life that's well-lived, too.** Our dream is not about perfection or some impractical or unreasonable ideal. The 28 needs that make up work well-being are not going to be thriving at the same time throughout your work life or in your workplace. Even getting your top 5 motives to be strong poses a challenge. What I do know is that motives should not be drowning, that stories of suffering motives like my mom's and mine and so many others I have heard along the way at Motives Met should be a thing of the past. What I do know is toxic workplaces and work relationships should be unacceptable. What I do know is that companies are built by their people, and they have a responsibility to care for their people's human needs. We all have a responsibility to care for motives at work if we want the future of work to be human.

Our dream is about the health and happiness that everyone deserves in a huge part of their lives, a dream that is attainable if we live by our Work Life Well-Lived Principles together. This dream will be made possible the more people we get to walk on the Motives Met Pathway with us, and I hope you will be one of them.

We are at a profound point in time to reimagine how we want to move forward and what we want the future of work to be, and each and every one of us plays a role. If you want to contribute to the work well-being movement, I would love it if you shared your action plan, motive stories, and experiences with us at motivesmet.com/human-work-world. How do you meet one of your motives in a way that could help others? What is something that has worked well for you in your work relationships? How do you or your company do a great job at meeting the motives of your people that others can learn from?

We will be collecting these ideas and stories and sharing them on our platform, in social media, and communication outreach to help us co-create well-being at work together. I look forward to hearing from you!

HEARTFELT THANKS

Thank you for journeying through these pages and being part of a better future of work. No matter where you are on your work well-being journey, may this book lead you toward your work life well-lived. If you found the book valuable and felt compelled to leave a review on Amazon or wherever you purchased your book, I would be very grateful. It helps other readers discover the book and further spread its message and impact in the world.

YOUR MOTIVES
MET HUMAN NEEDS
ASSESSMENT™ CODE

With the purchase of this book you will be provided a free code to the Motives Met Human Needs Assessment™ to discover your top 5 motives, along with your personal report.

Please visit this link to upload your information and receive your code. Or scan the QR code below.

motivesmet.com/code

CONNECT WITH KELLY AND MOTIVES MET

motivesmet.com

@kellymackin_motivesmet

in/KellyMackin

THE MOTIVES MET PLATFORM FOR LEADERS AND ORGANIZATIONS

We have developed many tangible tools and resources to help leaders take action toward creating their best workplace where people thrive and thus their business thrives. For more information, visit our website, motivesmet.com.

THE MOTIVES MET HUMAN NEEDS ASSESSMENT™

Bringing the Motives Met Assessment to your team or organization offers a multitude of benefits, as elaborated upon in this book. We make using the assessment simple, providing you with valuable tools such as an interactive motives dashboard, comprehensive team reports, and additional resources.

HUMAN CONNECTION SOFTWARE

The Motives Met Human Connection software is a powerful tool to have meaningful conversations that matter about motives and amplify psychological safety, trust, and connection. Our software accompanies the Motives Met Human Needs Assessment™ and provides a platform for personalized motive discussions, identifying goals and action plans to strengthen motives for your employees and in your culture.

MOTIVES MET WORKSHOPS

Post-assessment workshops provide an organization or team the opportunity to walk the Motives Met Pathway together. From creating and sharing motive stories to deepening human connection through motive exercises or developing ideas to better meet motives in your culture, our various workshop offerings are an impactful way to put insights into action.

LEADERSHIP COACHING, ONLINE PROGRAMS, AND CERTIFICATIONS

If you want to lead well-being and a people-first culture for your employees or your clients, we offer learning opportunities and certifications to give you all the knowledge and tools you need.

EMPLOYEE LEARNING AND WEBINARS

Whether through webinars or coaching sessions, we share the research, framework, and Work Life Well-Lived Principles to develop the shared Motives Mindset on your team or organization.

GRATITUDE

believe that the purpose of having big ambitions is not to reach a destination; it's about who you become in the process. Back in November of 2021, I dared to believe I had a book inside me, a message and mission that the world needed to hear. Yet the person I was then stands worlds apart from the person I am today: an almost-published author as I write these final words. I am grateful it has expanded me into a version of myself I have known deep down was possible.

I knew writing this book would be hard. I never could have anticipated just how hard. *Work Life Well-Lived* is a dream come true to that younger me who proclaimed in my mother's office that I was going to write a book one day. That dream would not have been possible, however, without the love and support of so many. I want to give a special thanks to a few specific people.

To my mother, thank you for going on this wild journey with me, for believing in me and the possibility for our hopes of a more human way of working. I admire what you were able to do in your work life and beyond, even with the obstacles standing in your way. To my entire family, my brother and sister, I am so grateful for your encouragement, unwavering confidence in me, and willingness to make never-ending book-related decisions over many months! Andy, your entrepreneurial advice and stories never cease to inspire. Thank you for your pep talks when I needed to hear them. Margaret, thank you for rolling up your sleeves and joining the Motives Met team when you did; you have been invaluable to say the least. Dad might not be toasting with us in person for this book launch, but I know he's dancing and singing to celebrate in spirit, and very proud.

This book and Motives Met would not be possible without my greatest mentor and leader of all time, brilliant researcher and overall inspiring soul Josh McQueen. Thank you doesn't seem adequate for all the ways you have inspired me and taught me over the years. Your vision and statistical genius was the spark that started it all, and it was an honor to be on the journey with you. I am eternally grateful for you more than you could ever know.

To all my friends near and far and the Motives Met team, I am so thankful for your support. Thank you, Catherine Cecil, for being my stand-in sister when my sister couldn't be here. Thank you to Andrew Urban, Katie Nicholl, and Maria Curtsinger for being some of my biggest book believers. To all my fellow Toastmasters, the confidence you give me is vital for enabling me to bring this into the world. I am so lucky I found you all. To the Motives Met clients, advocates, and people-first leaders, the world needs more people like you; keep leading the way to a future of work that is human. Marawan Aziz, I believe it was a gift from the powers that be that connected us. The platform and technology behind Motives Met wouldn't be possible without you and your dedication; a million thanks. Alex Brenner, you have been an incredible addition to the Motives Met team. Thank you for leading some of the Motives Met work that allowed me to take this book to the finish line. I also can't forget about the best writing buddy there ever was, my crazy pup, Dasher—you made "book lockdown" bearable and lay in my lap for countless hours as I wrote.

For all of the extremely talented publishing, editorial, and design team members at Greenleaf: HaJ, Erin Brown, Elizabeth Brown, Laurie MacQueen, Adrianna Hernandez, and Pam Nordberg, who jumped on making this book happen on a tight timeline, THANK YOU! A special shout out to the extraordinary designer Wes Henry who created the most beautiful brand for Motives Met that we were able to carry through into this book.

To all who have shared your motive stories with excitement, inspiration, and vulnerability, I appreciate you and look forward to hearing more motive stories from other readers.

NOTES

INTRODUCTION

1. Annie Dillard, *The Writing Life* (New York: HarperCollins, 1989).

2. Zach Mercurio, post on Linkedin, 2022, https://www.linkedin.com/feed/update/urn:li:activity:6962847673104154624?updateEntityUrn=urn%3Ali%3Afs_updateV2%3A%28urn%3Ali%3Aactivity%3A6962847673104154624%2CFEED_DETAIL%2CEMPTY%2CDEFAULT%2Cfalse%29.

3. Edward O. Wilson, *Consilience: The Unity of Knowledge* (New York: Alfred Knopf, 1998).

PART 1: THE WORK WELL-BEING MOVEMENT
CHAPTER 1: DREAMING OF A HUMAN WORK WORLD

1. Jack Kelly, "Wellbeing Is Just as Valuable to Workers as Their Pay, Study Finds," *Forbes*, October 18, 2023, https://www.forbes.com/sites/jackkelly/2023/10/18/wellbeing-is-just-as-valuable-to-workers-as-their-pay-study-finds/?utm_campaign=socialflowForbesMainLI&utm_medium=social&utm_source=ForbesMainLinkedIn&sh=4e0399d318dc.

2. "Great Expectations: Making Hybrid Work *Work*," Microsoft.com, March 16, 2022, https://www.microsoft.com/en-us/worklab/work-trend-index/great-expectations-making-hybrid-work-work#:~:text=In%20our%20study%2C%2047%25%20of,wellbeing%20over%20work%20than%20before.

3. Jocelyne Gafner, "The Impact of Workplace Wellbeing and How to Foster It," Indeed.com, updated April 26, 2023, https://www.indeed.com/career-advice/career-development/workplace-wellbeing.

4. Gafner, "Impact of Workplace Wellbeing."

5. "Workers Appreciate and Seek Mental Health Support in the Workplace," *American Psychological Association*, accessed October 19, 2023, https://www.apa.org/pubs/reports/work-well-being/2022-mental-health-support.

6. Steve Hatfield, Jen Fisher, and Paul H. Silverglate, "The C-Suite's Role in Well-Being," Deloitte Insights, June 22, 2022, https://www2.deloitte.com/us/en/insights/topics/leadership/employee-wellness-in-the-corporate-workplace.html.

7. Donald Sull and Charles Sull, "Toxic Culture Is Driving the Great Resignation," *MIT Sloan Management Review*, January 11, 2022, https://sloanreview.mit.edu/article/toxic-culture-is-driving-the-great-resignation/.

8. Colleen Bordeaux, Jen Fisher, and Anh Nguyen Phillips, "Why Reporting Workplace Well-Being Metrics Is a Good Idea," Deloitte Insights, June 21, 2022, https://www2.deloitte.com/us/en/insights/environmental-social-governance/employee-workplace-wellbeing-metrics.html.

9. Stephen Miller and Kathy Gurchiek, "Lonely at Work," SHRM, March 29, 2023, https://www.shrm.org/hr-today/news/all-things-work/pages/lonely-at-work.aspx.

10. Jim Harter, "U.S. Employee Engagement Needs a Rebound in 2023," Gallup.com, October 18, 2023, https://www.gallup.com/workplace/468233/employee-engagement-needs-rebound-2023.aspx.

11. Jon Clifton, "The World's Workplace Is Broken—Here's How to Fix It," Gallup.com, August 23, 2023, https://www.gallup.com/workplace/393395/world-workplace-broken-fix.aspx.

12. "Future Forum Pulse Winter Snapshot," Future Forum, February 15, 2023, https://futureforum.com/research/future-forum-pulse-winter-2022-2023-snapshot/.

CHAPTER 2: WHAT IS WORK WELL-BEING?

1. Daniel Wheatley, "Autonomy in Paid Work and Employee Subjective Well-Being," *Work and Occupations* 44, no. 3 (March 2017): 296–328, https://doi.org/10.1177/0730888417697232.

2. "GoodFirms Employee Engagement Survey Reveals: Globally Around 73.62% Workers Expect Opportunities for Growth at Job," Cision PR Newswire, January 21, 2020, https://www.prnewswire.com/news-releases/goodfirms -employee-engagement-survey-reveals-globally-around-73-62-workers-expect -opportunities-for-growth-at-job-300990206.html.

3. Karyn Twaronite, "The Surprising Power of Simply Asking Coworkers How They're Doing," *Harvard Business Review*, February 28, 2019, https:// hbr.org/2019/02/the-surprising-power-of-simply-asking-coworkers -how-theyre-doing.

4. "Breaking Boredom: Job Seekers Jumping Ship for New Challenges in 2018, According to Korn Ferry Survey," Korn Ferry, January 4, 2018, https://www .kornferry.com/about-us/press/breaking-boredom-job-seekers-jumping-ship -for-new-challenges-in-2018-according-to-korn-ferry-survey.

5. Tim Rath and Jim Harter, "Your Friends and Your Social Well-Being," Gallup .com, March 24, 2023, https://news.gallup.com/businessjournal/127043/friends -social-wellbeing.aspx.

6. Kim Parker and Juliana Menasce Horowitz, "Majority of Workers Who Quit a Job in 2021 Cite Low Pay, No Opportunities for Advancement, Feeling Disrespected," Pew Research Center, March 9, 2022, https://www.pewresearch .org/short-reads/2022/03/09/majority-of-workers-who-quit-a-job-in-2021 -cite-low-pay-no-opportunities-for-advancement-feeling-disrespected/.

7. Chris Schembra, "Gratitude May Be the Secret to Overcoming the Talent Crisis," Fast Company, August 13, 2021, https://www.fastcompany .com/90665927/gratitude-may-be-the-secret-to-overcoming-the-talent-crisis.

8. Grace He, "Happy Employee Statistics & Facts," Teambuilding.com, updated October 16, 2023, https://teambuilding.com/blog/happy-employee -statistics#:~:text=60%25%20of%20employees%20believe%20their,biggest%20 contribution%20to%20job%20happiness.

9. "Remote Work Is Linked to Happiness: Study of 12,455 Respondents," Tracking Happiness, updated June 18, 2023, https://www.trackinghappiness .com/remote-work-leads-to-happiness-study/.

10. Jennifer Schramm, "Respect and Trust Top the List of Most Important Employee Job Satisfaction Factors," SHRM (blog), May 1, 2015, https://blog.shrm.org/blog/ respect-and-trust-top-the-list-of-most-important-employee-job-satisfaction.

11. "Does Variety Fuel Happiness at Work and in Life? It Depends," Knowledge at Wharton, March 25, 2015, https://knowledge.wharton.upenn.edu/article/does-variety-fuel-happiness-at-work-and-in-life-it-depends/.

12. "Udemy Snapshot: 2019 Workplace Happiness Report," Udemy, accessed November 19, 2023, https://research.udemy.com/wp-content/uploads/2019/05/Workplace-Happiness-Report-2019-2021-Rebrand-v3-gs.pdf.

13. "Employees Don't Leave Companies, They Leave Managers," Sewells, accessed December 1, 2023, sewells.com/employees-dont-leave-companies-leave-managers/#:~:text=We've%20learned%20that%2075,reporting%20relationship%20isn't%20healthy.

14. Barbara Plester and Ann Hutchison, "Fun Times: The Relationship Between Fun and Workplace Engagement," *Employee Relations* 38, no. 3 (2016): 332–350, https://doi.org/10.1108/er-03-2014-0027.

15. Ben Wigert and Sangeeta Agrawal, "Employee Burnout, Part 1: The 5 Main Causes," Gallup.com, July 12, 2018, https://www.gallup.com/workplace/237059/employee-burnout-part-main-causes.aspx.

16. "Workers Value Meaning at Work; New Research from BetterUp Shows Just How Much They're Willing to Pay for It," BetterUp, November 7, 2018, https://www.betterup.com/press/workers-value-meaning-at-work-new-research-from-betterup-shows-just-how-much-theyre-willing-to-pay-for-it.

17. Tom Rath and Don Clifton, *StrengthsFinder 2.0* (Washington, DC: Gallup Press, 2017).

18. Gary Chapman and Paul White, *The 5 Languages of Appreciation in the Workplace* (Woodmere, NY: Northfield Publishing, 2019).

19. Stanford, "Steve Jobs 2005 Stanford Commencement Address," YouTube, March 7, 2008, accessed December 1, 2023, https://www.youtube.com/watch?v=UF8uR6Z6KLc.

20. "The Great Attrition or the Great Attraction: What Will It Be for You?" McKinsey & Company, October 13, 2021, https://www.mckinsey.com/featured-insights/mckinsey-live/webinars/the-great-attrition-or-the-great-attraction-what-will-it-be-for-you.

PART 2: THE MOTIVES MET PATHWAY
CHAPTER 4: WHY MOTIVES MATTER

1. Leah Weiss, *How We Work: Live Your Purpose, Reclaim Your Sanity, and Embrace the Daily Grind* (New York: HarperCollins, 2019).

2. Mike Robbins, "Are You Bringing Your Whole Self to Work?" Medium, April 30, 2018, https://mike-robbins.medium.com/ are-you-bringing-your-whole-self-to-work-ed7121ba20c1.

3. Daniel Goleman, *Emotional Intelligence: Why It Can Matter More Than IQ* (London: Bloomsbury, 1996).

4. Ludmila N. Praslova, "Practice Emotional Inclusion at Work, Not Toxic Positivity," *Psychology Today*, June 29, 2022, https:// www.psychologytoday.com/us/blog/positively-different/202206/ practice-emotional-inclusion-at-work-not-toxic-positivity.

5. Heidi Wachter, "Making Friends with Stress: Kelly McGonigal," Experience Life, February 25, 2016, https://experiencelife.lifetime.life/article/ making-friends-with-stress-kelly-mcgonigal/.

6. Nick Wignall, "4 Simple Habits for Peace of Mind," Medium, July 2, 2023, https://nickwignall.medium.com/4-simple-habits-for-peace-of-mind -f2517e7bb631.

7. Wigert and Agrawal, "Employee Burnout, Part 1."

8. "Burnout Is Caused by Mismatch between Unconscious Needs and Job Demands," ScienceDaily, August 11, 2016, https://www.sciencedaily.com/ releases/2016/08/160811171643.htm.

9. Jennifer Moss, *The Burnout Epidemic: The Rise of Chronic Stress and How We Can Fix It* (Boston: Harvard Business Review Press, 2021).

CHAPTER 5: MOTIVES MATTER FOR ORGANIZATIONS

1. Shane McFeely and Ben Wigert, "This Fixable Problem Costs U.S. Businesses $1 Trillion," Gallup.com, March 13, 2019, https://www.gallup.com/ workplace/247391/fixable-problem-costs-businesses-trillion.aspx.

2. "Essential Elements of Employee Retention," Lynchburg Regional SHRM, October 29, 2017, https://lrshrm.shrm.org/blog/2017/10/essential-elements-employee-retention.

3. Chase Charaba, "Employee Retention: The Real Cost of Losing an Employee," PeopleKeep, updated September 18, 2023, https://www.peoplekeep.com/blog/employee-retention-the-real-cost-of-losing-an-employee.

4. McFeely and Wigert, "This Fixable Problem."

5. McFeely and Wigert, "This Fixable Problem."

6. McFeely and Wigert, "This Fixable Problem."

7. Hatfield, Fisher, and Silverglate, "The C-Suite's Role," https://www2.deloitte.com/us/en/insights/topics/leadership/employee-wellness-in-the-corporate-workplace.html.

8. Amy C. Edmondson, *The Fearless Organization: Creating Psychological Safety in the Workplace for Learning, Innovation, and Growth* (Hoboken, NJ: Wiley, 2018).

CHAPTER 6: BECOMING MINDFUL TO MEET YOUR MOTIVES

1. Seth J. Gillihan, "Do You Know What You Need?" *Psychology Today*, July 27, 2015, https://www.psychologytoday.com/us/blog/think-act-be/201507/do-you-know-what-you-need.

2. Jim Collins, *Good to Great: Why Some Companies Make the Leap . . . and Others Don't* (New York: HarperBusiness, 2001).

CHAPTER 7: WELL-BEING IS CO-CREATED

1. Melissa Doman, *Yes, You Can Talk About Mental Health at Work: Here's Why (and How to Do It Really Well)* (London: Welbeck, 2020).

2. Jeffrey Pfeffer, "The Overlooked Essentials of Employee Well-Being," *McKinsey Quarterly*, September 2018, https://jeffreypfeffer.com/wp-content/uploads/2019/11/McKinsey-EmployeeHealth.pdf.

3. Sharon Salzberg, *Real Happiness: The Power of Meditation* (London: Hay House, 2020).

CHAPTER 9: CREATING YOUR MOTIVE STORY

1. Jonathan M. Adler, Jennifer Lodi-Smith, Frederick L. Philippe, Iliane Houle, "The Incremental Validity of Narrative Identity in Predicting Well-Being: A Review of the Field and Recommendations for the Future," *Personality and Social Psychology Review* 20, no. 2 (May 2016): 142–175, doi:10.1177/1088868315585068.

CHAPTER 10: TALKING ABOUT WHAT MATTERS MOST

1. Leslie K. John, "The Surprising Power of Questions," *Harvard Business Review,* May–June 2018, https://hbr.org/2018/05/the-surprising-power-of-questions.

2. K. A. Duffy and T. L. Chartrand, "The Extravert Advantage: How and When Extraverts Build Rapport with Other People," *Psychological Science* 26, no. 11, 1795–1802, doi: 10.1177/0956797615600890.

3. Barbara Field, "How Storytelling Is Good for Your Mental Health," Verywell Mind, November 17, 2021, https://www.verywellmind.com/how-storytelling-is-good-for-your-mental-health-5199744.

4. Kim Scott, *Radical Candor: Be a Kick-Ass Boss Without Losing Your Humanity* (New York: St. Martin's Griffin, 2017).

CHAPTER 11: PRIORITIZING YOUR HEALTH AND HAPPINESS AT WORK . . . *REALLY* PRIORITIZING IT

1. Email to the author, January 16, 2022.

2. "Why Celebrating Successes Is Important to Our Mental Health," Innovative Resources, August 11, 2021, https://innovativeresources.org/why-celebrating-successes-is-important-to-our-mental-health/#:~:text=A%20number%20of%20studies%20have,tend%20to%20be%20less%20stressed.

PART 3: THE MOTIVES MET PATHWAY FOR LEADERS
CHAPTER 13: LEADING THE WAY TO A
MORE HUMAN WORKPLACE

1. Dena Denham Smith and Alicia A. Grandey, "The Emotional Labor of Being a Leader," *Harvard Business Review*, November 2, 2022, https://hbr.org/2022/11/the-emotional-labor-of-being-a-leader.

CHAPTER 14: CO-CREATING A CULTURE OF WELL-BEING

1. TED, James Rhee, "The value of kindness at work| TED," YouTube, February 13, 2022, https://www.youtube.com/watch?v=sRoqDVgFgSw.

2. Nathan Podsakoff, Steven W. Whiting, Philip M. Podsakoff, and Brian D. Blume, "Individual- and Organizational-Level Consequences of Organizational Citizenship Behaviors: A Meta-Analysis," *Journal of Applied Psychology* 94, no. 1 (2009): 122–141, https://doi.org/10.1037/a0013079.

3. Gary Vaynerchuk, "Why Being Kind Is More Important Than Skill," LinkedIn post, accessed October 29, 2023, https://www.linkedin.com/posts/garyvaynerchuk_this-is-how-you-can-build-a-great-culture-activity-7026224870405369856-ws3P?utm_source=share&utm_medium=member_desktop.

4. Adam M. Grant, *Give and Take: Why Helping Others Drives Our Success* (New York: Penguin, reprint 2014).

CHAPTER 16: BEGINNING A NEVER-ENDING
CONVERSATION AROUND MOTIVES

1. Peter Brace, email to author, March 4, 2023.

2. Caroline Castrillon, "How to Handle Difficult Conversations at Work," *Forbes*, October 24, 2021, https://www.forbes.com/sites/carolinecastrillon/2021/10/24/how-to-handle-difficult-conversations-at-work/.

3. Patrick Lencioni, *The Five Dysfunctions of a Team: A Leadership Fable* (Hoboken, NJ: Jossey-Bass, 2002).

4. Monty Moran, *Love Is Free. Guac Is Extra.: How Vulnerability, Empowerment, and Curiosity Built an Unstoppable Team* (Carson City, NV: Lioncrest, 2020).

CHAPTER 17: COMMITTING TO PUTTING PEOPLE FIRST

1. Eve Glicksman, "Report: Managers Have Bigger Impact on Employee Mental Health Than Therapists," SHRM, February 15, 2023, https://www.shrm.org/resourcesandtools/hr-topics/employee-relations/pages/manager-mental-health-of-employees.aspx.

CHAPTER 18: CREATING YOUR PEOPLE-FIRST ACTION PLAN

1. TEDxTalks, "The Future of Work | JEN FISHER | TEDxMiami," YouTube, July 27, 2023, https://www.youtube.com/watch?v=M9l_lpYnzhI.

ABOUT THE AUTHOR

Kelly Mackin is the cofounder and CEO of the Motives Met Platform, which includes actionable tools like the Motives Met Human Needs Assessment™ and Human Connection software to empower people to create their best work life and workplace. Kelly's journey from ill-being to well-being at work ignited her passion for helping people create health and happiness in their lives through a unique blend of skills.

As a quantitative researcher of human behavior, she gains insights into significant parts of life like values, stress, and emotions to develop frameworks to better understand the world and ourselves to make positive change. A forever student of learning about our human brains and the science of how we think, she is an accredited mind management, psychological safety, and cognitive behavioral therapy coach. She also draws on her experience as a meditation teacher to use mindfulness-based practices to improve life in our modern world in and outside of work. In her coaching practice, she helped her clients with anxiety, burnout prevention, and mindset training.

Kelly's mission is to create a human work world, and she built Motives Met to achieve the attainable dream of a work life well-lived for all. When asked about her proudest moments, Kelly would tell you it was standing at the top of Mount Kilimanjaro in Africa and at Mount Everest Base Camp. Hailing from sunny San Diego, California, you can often find her soaking up a sunset, playing beach volleyball, or sparring in the boxing ring.

CONNECT WITH KELLY AND MOTIVES MET

📍   motivesmet.com

📷   @kellymackin_motivesmet

in   in/KellyMackin